MW00679658

MEDITATIONS FOR ALCOHOLICS AND THEIR FAMILIES

edited by
Judy Osgood

GILGAL PUBLICATIONS
P.O. Box 3399
Sunriver, OR 97707
(503) 593-8418   FAX: (503) 593-5604

Copyright © 1993 by Gilgal Publications

All rights reserved - no part of this book may be reproduced in any form without permission in writing from the publisher, except by a reviewer who wishes to quote brief passages in connection with a review written for inclusion in a magazine or newspaper.

Library of Congress Cataloging-in-Publication Data

Meditations for alcoholics and their families / edited by Judy Osgood.
    p.   cm. ---- (Gilgal meditation series)
  ISBN 0-916895-04-1
  1. Alcoholics----Prayer books and devotions----English. I. Osgood,
Judy. II. Series.
  BL625.9.A43M43   1993
  242' .4----dc20   92-41267
                                                         CIP

ISBN 0-916895-04-1

Printed in the United States of America.

Some of the names in this book have been changed.

Cover Photo by David Osgood

Other books in the Gilgal Meditation Series:

MEDITATIONS FOR BEREAVED PARENTS

MEDITATIONS FOR THE WIDOWED

MEDITATIONS FOR THE DIVORCED

MEDITATIONS FOR THE TERMINALLY ILL AND THEIR FAMILIES

CONTENTS

"It is only when you have been burned to ashes that you completely find God. Then when everything in you seems to have been extinguished, a new little flame is somehow lighted, which grows and grows and can never be put out. That flame is God"

Anonymous
The Interpreter's Bible
Volume 1, Page 767

IN THE END IT WAS SOUL SICKNESS

How like herrings and onions our vices are the morning after we have committed them. . .

Samuel Taylor Coleridge

The hangovers, oh, the hangovers! The churning stomach, the head made of lead, the thumbs that quivered, all accompanied by an eerie feeling of disembodiment.

But even worse was the soul sickness, which included remorse over what I had done, when I could remember what it was, or when I couldn't remember, a chilling fear of what I might have done. Where had I been, and with whom? How did I get home? I still remember clawing through wallet, purse and clothing looking for clues to events that the brain had failed to record.

The title of Florence King's autobiography accurately describes what I was - a failed southern lady. When quite young, I was often referred to as "a nice girl," which may have been the start of my problem, as the description set me apart from many of my peers. I didn't want to be a nice girl; I wanted to be like the ones who were having fun. While I don't know what became of them, I know what became of me. I became an alcoholic.

11

After graduation, I went to work as a secretary. Vowing to behave myself, I only got drunk on weekends. I married a man who also only got drunk on weekends, and a year later a baby boy arrived. If there's anything a drunk hates, it's responsibility. Soon we were drinking more, fighting a lot, and the marriage ended in divorce.

I got a better-paying job, but it was boring. Another thing a drunk hates is boredom. I was not closely supervised, so I began to drink heavily during the week, and often wore dark glasses at the office to hide my bloodshot eyes. No one seemed to notice. Now the hangovers were so severe that I took an occasional nip from a bottle I kept in a file drawer.

One night after work I met a man in a bar. He wasn't much to look at and had no polish, but we became drinking soul mates. We met at the bar each evening, and things worsened at the office. Only my resignation to get married saved me from dismissal.

After the wedding he took me and my son to his hometown, which proved to be a hamlet in the backwoods of Virginia. Soon my second son was born. By this time my husband and I couldn't stand each other, I couldn't stand his hometown, and we rarely drew a sober breath. The hangovers were daily, and the soul sickness was always with me.

I knew a normal wife and mother didn't go through life falling-down drunk, but by then I was truly addicted. The knowledge of what I should be, contrasted with what I was, kept me in a state of anguish, but I seemed powerless to change.

Though alcohol was ravaging my body, in the end it was the soul sickness that brought me to my knees. I always knew there was a God, but I never thought of asking Him to save me from the consequences of my own actions until I reached the point where there was simply nowhere else to turn.

It has been years now since I left the Virginia hamlet, got my second divorce and had my last drink. Only in complete surrender to a loving God, who sent me the help I needed, was I able to emerge victorious from the deep, dark pit of alcoholism.

Thank you, God, for allowing me to become sick enough so I could begin to get well.

Nancy

THE UNACKNOWLEDGED ALCOHOLIC

Skid row and its victims remain, providing the other 95 percent of America's alcoholics with a visible, sordid, and highly acceptable rationalization for the continuing denial of their own illness.
Jack B. Weiner

My father died when I was fourteen. His death resolved the problem we never dealt with as a family. The tragedy was that for the entirety of our lives together, there was a bottle between us. If he knew he was an alcoholic, he never admitted it. I guess my mother and I knew it and didn't understand it, but we were unquestionably victims of his alcoholism.

We did not have a violent household nor a financially insecure one. It was more remote, with vague undercurrents of tension. There was a small static charge like the kind that makes you wary about reaching for a worn lamp switch. It was always there; never dangerous, just disturbing.

There were, as well, many happy times and no serious apprehensions that drinking was going to jeopardize our family, our future or our lifestyle. My father did not go on binges, stumble home drunk, or abandon the house to sit in bars. He never drove while drinking, never missed a day of work and never failed to provide for his family's security and comfort.

The signs of his drinking were subtle. They showed up in his personality making him irritable, belligerent, argumentative, critical, impossible to please and unpleasant to be around.

In my adult life I did not consider my own drinking to be an indication of alcoholism. I got mellow, not "drunk." I didn't drink alone, didn't miss work and I didn't suffer hangovers. And I successfully convinced myself that I was a social drinker until a cancer diagnosis coupled with the financial, career and psychological problems that came with it triggered a brooding, alcoholic withdrawal that lasted over a year and contributed to a near suicidal depression. It took months and months of intense professional counselling to restore a normal perspective.

I don't know what causes alcoholism, but I know it isn't opening bottles. An alcoholic is an alcoholic before the cap is off. Maybe it's a matter of not knowing where to look for courage or strength or comfort. Maybe it's a substitute for looking. Whatever it is, it grows until it blinds, cripples and kills its host; or until its host purges himself of it. My father did not see it in time. I did.

God, thank you for giving me a warning while I was still able to see it.

Pete

A FAMILY LEGACY

You shall give life to things but never possess them.
Lao Tzu

As the wife of a successful attorney and mother of three beautiful children, I was caught up in the privileged life. I really thought I had it all until a thief called alcoholism began stealing everything from me.

At first I noticed the thief's symptoms in my husband; later, in myself. By then we were both on a downward slide that culminated in alcoholic fights and an ugly divorce with a custody battle which my husband won.

Alone in the world and on my own, I used alcohol to numb the pain and enormous anger I felt over my loss. Life, indeed, had become unbearable on my terms. With nowhere else to turn I sought help in Alcoholics Anonymous, and there I eventually found hope.

However, my fragile progress was almost consumed in the fire of renewed hatred and anger I felt toward my former husband when I learned that our 14-year-old-son, Daniel was also an alcoholic. My feelings were so intense that I was afraid I would lose my hard won sobriety. To cope with that I switched to automatic, and following my AA sponsor's suggestions, I went to extra meetings, talked about my problems and feelings, and even went for counselling.

In return, the understanding of so many friends, the patience of my sponsors, and the wisdom of my therapist brought me to the realization, finally, that yes, my young teenaged son could be an alcoholic. I had contributed in large part to that legacy, but had no power to control the outcome.

Because I understood that God alone could help him, I prayed a lot. Initially, I challenged God asking, "How could you let this happen?" but as time went on I learned to say instead, "Thy will be done."

As I prayed for him, I also worked at my own recovery and on changing myself. For two years Daniel and I struggled with our individual recovery programs and tried to put together a new and honest parent-child relationship. Liberation came for me when I was able to let go and finally forgive my son and my former husband.

My efforts were rewarded not long ago when Daniel called and said, "Mom, I think I'd like to come and live with you."

Today I have something of value to offer my son and that is one of the best benefits of recovery. My heart is full and I weep tears of joy for I've been given a second chance at the sacred trust of motherhood.

Dear God, please give me the grace and courage to become the mother I was meant to be.

Emilie

14

MY WIFE CAN'T BE AN ALCOHOLIC!

". . . you will know the truth, and the truth will set you free."
John 8:32 (TLB)

In retrospect, I am appalled at my refusal to see reality . . .

I was sure my wife was out to ruin me. Although I rarely saw her drink, it seemed as if she was always drunk. Our checks were returned for insufficient funds, the grocery money was spent for booze, our living room drapes were never open, newspaper was taped over our bedroom windows because the light bothered her eyes, and the neighbors watched out for our son. Frankly, I didn't know how much more I could take, but I still couldn't admit why all this was happening.

The day my wife informed me that she was an alcoholic and that she was going to a recovery home for several months, my ego suffered a devastating blow. I could handle her frequent short hospitalizations for "nervous breakdowns," but to have my wife be an alcoholic was totally unthinkable. My pride would not stand for such a thing. Even I could see that she drank too much, but she wasn't that bad.

Assuming my Pastor would agree with me and that he would have some good advice on how to help my wife deal with her problem, I went to him for a little counselling. But he didn't agree with me. What he told me was that I should work on my own faults and let her correct her own. I left his office feeling very angry and downright indignant. She was the one with the problem, not me. Hadn't I covered her bad checks and held our home together while she was drinking? That, I figured, made me the "good guy" and it was she who needed to change.

Rage fueled my trip home, but it subsided when I finally gave in to years of pent up anxiety and let the tears flow. After I'd calmed down, I began to pray and as I did so, I became aware of the self-pity I had wallowed in for longer than I cared to think about. I saw the martyr I tried so hard to be, and realized how badly I had deceived myself.

I'd been blaming her for all our problems, even the ones I caused. Her struggle to get free of the grip that the disease of alcoholism had on her was something I could not yet comprehend. That would come with time. What I did know then was that despite her behavior, despite her addiction, I still loved her very deeply and I knew that she needed me more then than she ever had before.

To help her, to help us, I made a vow to work on my own shortcomings and to support her any way I could, as she tackled her own problems.

Thank you, Father, for the truth that sets us free and for the wisdom to keep building a better tomorrow on the mistakes of yesterday.

Merle

IF HE REALLY LOVED ME

Courage is fear that has said its prayers.
Karle Wilson Baker

I used to think if that man really loved me, he'd quit drinking. It was his decision to take that first drink and I told myself he could also choose to take his last.

As I struggled with the behavior of my alcoholic, I found myself evaluating my own conduct and wondering if I was causing the conflict. One by one I examined my own faults and either accepted or rejected them.

For 30 years I'd been a smoker, but I wouldn't have become addicted if I had never taken that first cigarette. Nor would I have become overweight if I hadn't lifted food to my mouth in excess - one spoonful at a time.

It was my own responsibility to quit smoking or continue to light up, and my choice to overeat or not. I, alone, was liable for any adverse affects on my health and no one forced my decision.

Working through my personal tally sheet eventually brought me to a listing called, "Willingness to accept unacceptable behavior in others." I knew I could not be the person I wanted to be and continue to cower under verbal abuse and constant crisis. And so I cried out, "No more!"

The time for detachment had come. Again, I was accountable because no one could do it for me. I had to look at my situation realistically and objectively to make intelligent decisions, and I had to understand that I wasn't responsible for his drinking, nor was I responsible for his recovery.

From there I turned to God in prayer. While I knew that alcoholism could not be prayed away or wished away, I found that God could guide me to lead a happier and more manageable life. He gave me the courage to attend Al-Anon, the courage to remain with my alcoholic, and the courage to refuse to be manipulated or abused.

Thank you, Father, that the courage which comes from you is unfailing.

Barbara

THIS THING CALLED "GRACE"

Grace is the central invitation to life, and the final word. It's the beckoning nudge and the overwhelming, undeserved mercy which urges us to change and grow, and then gives us the power to pull it off.
Tim Hansel

Our home environment was a physically and emotionally abusive one, influenced by alcoholism. My earliest memories are of my mother being taken to the hospital by ambulance after being beaten by my father. About all I can recall of my childhood are the weekends of constant screaming and yelling.

Like other children of alcoholics, I somehow learned that if I were to be a better person and a "good girl" that none of this unhappiness would exist, and I've spent a lifetime coming to grips with the effects of that false guilt.

I grew up not knowing if I could ever bring friends home because I was unsure of what the atmosphere of the moment would be, or what I would find when I got there. One day, for example, I returned from school to find my father's clothes thrown out a window and into a snow bank. No child wants their classmates to see something like that.

As the oldest of three children it was my task to decide which parent all of us would live with during the frequent separations. It was always a lose-lose situation for no matter which I chose, the other would denounce my decision.

During my teenage years I began acting out, screaming at the smallest of things, demanding my own way, and generally being pretty awful to everyone. Confusion and turmoil were a way of life for me for I was consumed with bitterness and hate.

During my sophomore year in college I came home to help my parents move to a new city. One evening my Mother found me putting the younger kids to bed. She was upset with Dad who had left to attend his first AA meeting and yelled at me, saying I was the blame for all our family's discord. In her rage she pushed me down a flight of stairs, then called nearby relatives and the police and told them I had tried to kill her. The police dismissed the incident and told us to calm down.

When my Father returned later than evening, I told him the story, but I never knew if he believed me or not. Then and always, it seemed, I felt desperate and my sense of aloneness was so overwhelming I thought I was going crazy.

For years I held each bitter memory as a precious jewel to savor and remember, dwelling on each beating I received and remembering each time I was verbally abused. That evidence convinced me I was less than worthless and would never have a friend.

In retrospect, I realize that what I needed then was a fresh perspective that would give me the courage to put aside the painful past and build a satisfying life for myself. That need was met one day at church when I heard the Priest say, "God has enough grace for each of you, more than you will ever need."

If there is a more difficult Christian term to define than "grace," I don't know what it is, for it is at the same time God's forgiveness and the unlimited possibilities his love provides for each of us.

Another day that comment might have meant little or nothing to me, but that day it was precisely what I needed to hear for I had given up on myself and was convinced I was not o.k. His choice of words quite literally meant a chance for a new life for me. I seized on those thoughts, began to feel much less alone, and reached out for counselling and support.

Following many years of hard work and growth I learned that despite all the frightening and painful times, my parents were doing the very best they could. Before they died I was able to say "I forgive you" to each of them and really mean it. I also asked forgiveness for my terrible thoughts and behavior.

My parting gift to each of my parents when they died was a letter in their caskets, recounting our lives together and affirming my love and acceptance.

Lord, thank you for the grace to know forgiveness and set aside my bitterness.

Rita

LEARNING TO READ GOD'S SIGNS

Signs are seen by the eyes of faith; they are visible to no other.
Edward R. Sims

I told myself I was just a social drinker who could take it or leave it because I was in complete control. At least I thought I was until one Friday evening when I discovered that it was the other way around and alcohol had control of me.

My husband and I had planned all week to visit good friends who lived forty miles away, but when Friday came he was so tired he didn't want to go. Instead of being understanding of the fact he had worked hard all week to support us, I convinced myself I was justified in going without him and left him home while I went in search of a good time.

At the club I enjoyed being with our friends. We talked about the latest best selling books and the political problems of the world, and I tried a few new dance steps. My friends assured me that if I drank too much I could ride home with them. Consequently I didn't worry about the drinks I was consuming like water. I was having the time of my life until . . .

. . . a small white dog darted across the road. When I stepped on the brakes my car turned around and stopped in the other lane of traffic. I looked behind me to see if I could back up safely, saw the flashing blue lights of a police car, and knew I was in trouble.

It was while I was sitting in a small solitary jail cell waiting for my husband that reality hit me and I began shaking with fear. I couldn't remember leaving the club, starting the car, or anything else that had happened during the last two hours, yet for some unknown reason I found myself recalling very clearly Father Ralph's sermon on Learning to Read God's Signs. It was our pastor's theory that God touches us in many ways and that we needed to be aware of what God was trying to tell us. That night God's message to me was so clear he might as well have painted a giant sign that said, "You've got a drinking problem, Pam."

Nor was that all He had to tell me. My husband's response to my trouble was so loving and helpful that I realized for the first time he wasn't just talking when he said he loved me. He really did.

On Monday morning I sent off a thank-you note to the policeman who arrested me because I was so appreciative of the fact he stopped me before anyone got hurt. And I am trying to make my life a thank-you note to God and my husband as I learn, with their help, to leave alcohol alone.

Thank you, Father, for sending us signs for guidance.

Pam

LITTLE FIBS, BIG LIES, AND UNADORNED TRUTH

You can't pray a lie.
Huckleberry Finn by Mark Twain

There were three rules in the alcoholic family I grew up in: Don't talk, don't feel, don't trust. But since no group of people, no matter how sick, can be totally silent with each other, we developed a unique style of communication. We lied.

Our measure of worth within the family was success; particularly success in the face of overwhelming odds. If we had triumphed in our daily activities, it was o.k. to share that and be rewarded as befits the victor in an insurmountable struggle. It made the family look and feel good.

If my successes throughout the day were mundane and easily achieved, they carried no weight around the dinner table. So I learned quickly to embellish them with over-statement and exaggeration. In order to justify my tales of power, my little league football team would have had to compete with the Pittsburgh Steelers.

The embellishments quickly turned into pure fabrications. Although we talked about lying as a sin, actuality proved otherwise. Perception became distorted as I looked at each situation with an eye toward how it would sound around the dinner table. Soon I was actually seeing things not as they were, but as I wanted them to be. Reality had been lost in the urge to please.

Whereas I had learned that a lie worked better than the truth in my family, at AA I learned that the "truth will set me free" in sobriety. AA's Twelve-Step recovery program is based on rigorous honesty and when I joined that group I quickly discovered that the only person there affected by my falsehoods was me.

Early on I even lied to my Higher Power in prayer and it took some time for me to see that only that which I prayed for in truth was answered. Eventually I discovered that it's just like Huckleberry Finn said, "You can't pray a lie." And he might have added, "It won't do you any good anyway because God will know the difference."

Today I am not saddled by the burdens of my lies. To me, the freedom in the concrete truth is best felt by the simple statement that starts us on our way to recovery, "My name is Ed; I am an alcoholic."

Thank You, God, for the freedom to become me, the real me, without any embellishments.

Ed

THE GAMES WE PLAYED

Honesty is the first chapter of the book of wisdom.
Thomas Jefferson

My alcoholic husband and I played a great many games during his drinking years and it seemed as though he always knew just what to do in order to get a desired reaction out of me. He acted one way and I, in turn, reacted exactly as he expected me to.

One incident in particular really opened my eyes to the fact that I was the one who set myself up for many of the disappointments I faced. It happened on a day when I was fed up with my husband's drinking and had once again lost my temper and blown up at him, making a threat I had no intention of following through on.

In response to my threat, my husband promised to quit drinking. As usual I got my hopes up, thinking that maybe this time he really was sincere.

By the end of the week, however, he was drunk again. I screamed at him and he screamed right back. Sarcastically he told me he'd had no intention of quitting, he'd only stopped long enough to get me off his back.

"How could I have been so stupid to fall for one of his lies again?" I wondered. "When was I ever going to learn I couldn't believe what he said?" Then the truth hit home. He couldn't believe me either.

I'd allowed my anger to get the best of me and given him an ultimatum I had no intention of keeping. He knew I'd never follow through on my threat; I never did. The whole scene was just another game we played that no one ever won.

If my husband was ever going to take me seriously, I had to learn to be totally honest, not only with him, but myself as well. And armed with that knowledge, I began the life-long process of evaluating my own responses to be sure I was honest with myself as well as with him.

Thank you, Lord, for teaching me that playing games accomplishes nothing.

Melanie

DON'T PULL AN ELVIS ON ME!

Oh Lord, thou hast searched me and known me!
Psalms 139:1 (RSV)

"I'll never drink!" At 17 I could make confident statements. At 20 one drink meant at least three. By age 30 I had a husband, two children and a worry - my drinking. Each day at 4:30 I started the cocktail hour, which lasted until we ate, around 7:00 p.m. A few years later I switched to a 5:00 p.m. starting time because I didn't want to be an alcoholic.

When we would go out for the evening, if I were absolutely positive liquor would be available, I'd make myself wait until we arrived; if I wasn't sure, I'd down three drinks before leaving home.

On March 17, 1972 I renewed my commitment to Jesus Christ as my Lord and Savior. From that time on I found I could share with others about the Lord's work in my life. But although I grew spiritually, my drinking progressed too. It wasn't until August 18, 1977 that I was uncomfortable enough with my behavior and scared enough about my health that I could ask my friends for help through their prayers.

Even though I'd asked, I wasn't sure if I wanted to go through the rest of my life without a drink. The next day, as I struggled internally, I thought about giving my gin to my neighbor Nancy, who had once loaned me some. Although I decided not to, I wanted to keep busy at 5:00 o'clock to avoid temptation, so I took my dog for a walk and promptly ran into Nancy. Instead of saying hello, she greeted me with, "What about that gin you owe me?" That not-too-terribly-subtle nudge from God took the decision out of my hands, and I gave her all that I had without any explanation.

An hour later an acquaintance phoned to say that a mutual friend had died suddenly from cirrhosis. She was 42 years old while I was 41-1/2. At my marketing research job the next morning I concluded a three minute interview with, "Thank you for your help, your opinion counts, and do have a good day." The response from that unknown woman on the other end of the line was startling. "You have a good day, too, sweetheart, and don't pull an Elvis on me." "Pardon?" I asked, not believing my ears. "Don't pull an Elvis on me," the stranger said, "don't die on me." Elvis Presley had died several days earlier at 42.

Awed and overwhelmed by how personally the Lord works, I knew he wanted me alive and sober. I no longer had a choice. It hasn't been easy and it's been one day at a time, but I haven't had a drink since.

My Lord, who searches and knows me, thank you for being an intimate part of my life.

Patricia

MAMA WAS A SOCIAL DRINKER

". . . I am not alone, for the Father is with me."
John 16:32 (RSV)

I knew even as a child that my Mama was a social drinker. By the time I was in my teens I realized she was an alcoholic and I also knew what to expect at her parties. With an arm wrapped around my neck, leaning her weight against me, she would tell all her friends what a wonderful daughter I was. Then with bleary eyes she would gaze at me and slur, "I'll give you anything you want." But I never took advantage of her offer because I knew she was drunk.

My mother has always been loving, kind, and generous. In the beginning her personality remained the same, drunk or sober. It wasn't until later that her personality changed to rudeness and cruelty when she was inebriated. She lost friends, respect, and a thirty-five year marriage. Today Mama is still an alcoholic on a destructive road which I believe will eventually kill her.

Did I ever become angry or impatient with my mother? You bet.

Do I ever feel alone? Many times.

Do I cry? Buckets full.

When I'm at the depths of despair about my mother's drinking problem, I cry out to God for help. During those times, God assures me that I'm not alone and that He's crying too. He loves my mother and died for her, just as He died for me. And knowing that he loves her too, how can I do less?

Thank you, Lord, for assuring me that you love my Mama too.

Beajay

THE ONLY TRUE SOLUTION

With men it is impossible, but not with God: for with God all things are possible.

Mark 10:27 (KJV)

I don't remember when drinking first became a problem because for a long time a drink or two was my solution. It dissolved stress, anger and worry; it softened feelings of inadequacy and fear. In fact, I remember kneeling in prayer one day and thanking God for providing me with a solution that seemed to work for everything so consistently and well. But that was long ago.

Once, in a movie I saw the hero board a merry-go-round. All was bright lights and tinkling music, when suddenly there was a mechanical breakdown. The big wheel began picking up speed, and by the time he realized the danger, it was spinning too fast for him to get off.

That's the way it was with my drinking. My precious solution slowly, gradually, deteriorated into a problem more devastating than anything I could have imagined.

Desperately I began searching for an answer.

"I will never take more than two drinks, I vowed, yet I always did. "I will stop drinking completely!" I proclaimed, but I couldn't. "Maybe a study of psychology would provide the answer," I thought, so I enrolled in a local college, but to no avail. "Hypnosis does wonders," someone said, but I tried it and it didn't. I also talked to various counsellors and a psychiatrist, but no one gave me a solution that worked.

As a last resort I committed myself into a state hospital, prepared to die. Yet it was there, on a magical November night, that everything changed. Following a therapy session, I was walking alone across the deserted hospital grounds toward my Unit. All at once I felt I wasn't alone. Someone, walking beside me, had brushed against my arm. I turned, but no one was there. As I stood, frozen, a feeling of peace such as I had never before experienced began to pour through me. I knew then that the Lord was there and everything would be all right.

The program of Alcoholics Anonymous talks about the healing power of a spiritual experience. That is what happened to me that night. At the eleventh hour I discovered the only true Solution, and He has been with me now for almost 18 years. Sometimes strangers remark on the kind of will power that results in long-term abstinence from alcohol. I never hesitate to set them straight. "Not will power," I answer. "There is only one solution to such a problem and that is God-Power."

Thank you, Father, for doing for me what I could never have done for myself.

Doris

HIS AND HER ILLNESSES

Those who cannot remember the past are condemned to repeat it.
George Santayana

"I have a hidden infection under scars that barely show. It lies in remission for awhile, then without warning, gushes from the shadows of loneliness, oozing heartbreak and renewed anxiety to every sensitive area of my life. My disease is called 'co-alcoholism.' I am as addicted to my alcoholic as he is addicted to the booze.

"I believe my alcoholic's lies, call his boss with excuses, hold a job to pay the bills, have him thrown in jail and then bail him out. I even pray for him.

"My world is not sane but I don't know how or where to get off."

Thousands of women participate in the above complaints and accept their marriage as a mutual failure until death comes: either his or hers.

My husband's death came first and my biggest sorrow was my absence of grief. Yet a year later when I began to date and became fond of a trusted widowed friend, I found myself in companionship with another alcoholic.

Statistics show that if the alcoholic dies and the co-alcoholic survivor goes untreated, he or she will often marry an alcoholic again and not even realize it until it's too late. That is also true of those who divorce an alcoholic.

As a co-alcoholic, I did not get well in the absence of my alcoholic husband. My illness had to be treated by professional counselling, love and acceptance from my family, and my own willingness to learn a new way of life. It also took time to learn that a lasting relationship is possible only with a person who is kind and willing to give of himself.

Because I am attracted to needy people, my tendency has been to plunge headlong into an attempt to prove my worth by becoming that person's counsellor and caretaker. That pattern made it difficult for me to accept that I had value and that two people must be good for each other. But God stuck with me until I learned that lesson, and knowing He was always there caring kept me from giving up on myself.

God also helps me to remember the past so I am not tempted to repeat it. I've learned that when praying, "...lead us not into temptation," I must not deliberately place myself in a position to be tempted if I want normal, happy, healthy relationships.

Thank you, Father, for saving me from another disastrous co-dependency relationship and for helping me to change my ways.

Barbara

STEP ONE: BELIEVE THE DIAGNOSIS

An alcoholic's recovery is usually connected to his ability to perceive his addiction as a disease.
Anderson Spickard, M.D.

My wife found it hard to believe that she had a drinking problem because her concept of an alcoholic was a falling-down drunk. And I found it hard to believe because I thought alcoholism was strictly a psychological problem and she seemed very well-adjusted to me. However, her enlarged liver was mute testimony to the fact that she did indeed have a problem created by scotch, and her doctor ultimately convinced us we were both wrong.

Lorraine was in the hospital battling an ulcer when our doctor confronted her and refused to release her until she accepted the fact she was an alcoholic and agreed to enter a residential recovery program.

When I checked her into the New Life House, I told her, "This is our problem and you and I are going to walk hand and hand through this thing together." While that calmed her fears for the moment, it wasn't long before she was sure I had forgotten her. What she didn't realize was that after I signed her in that first day the Program Supervisor told me, "Don't you dare show up here for 10 days."

Two days into the program she started calling and begging me to bring her home. Even now it's hard to talk about it as those days were excruciating. Her pleas were like a knife cutting into my heart. When they became unbearable I turned to our minister for moral support.

He didn't deny my pain or hers, nor did he offer platitudes to make me feel better. What he basically told me was that I had to have faith in what they were doing and I had to recognize that their counsel was much bigger than my emotions. He also said that in order to walk with her hand in hand, I had to overcome my emotions.

With his help I learned to trust the process. I tried to take in all the sessions for family members so I would have a better understanding of what she was going through, what to expect when she returned home, and how I could best help her.

Was it easy? No. Was it worth it? Yes. Lorraine managed to stay away from alcohol all the rest of her life and while I know her recovery may seem easier than most because she didn't slip, I also know that she was no different from any other alcoholic. Once she accepted the fact she had a disease called alcoholism, she knew she could never, ever drink another drop, and she didn't.

Thank you, Father, for helping us learn to live with alcoholism.

George

SHALL I LEAVE, OR SHALL I STAY?

People are about as happy as they decide they're going to be.
Abraham Lincoln

It usually takes several years for us to realize we are married to an alcoholic. We normally pass through the stages of denial, anger, covering up, and out-and-out combat with the disease before we are ready to admit we are involved in a problem too big to handle alone.

When I eventually went to Al-Anon, I learned there were hundreds of others worse off than I was, and I had an overpowering urge to run away before my situation deteriorated any more.

Many marriages do break up because of alcoholism, and it's possible that might be the best decision for all concerned. But because I had invested thirty-five years in ours, I decided I would carefully analyze the advantages and disadvantages of such a move before I made it. I spent many long hours listing the pros and cons. When I took stock of all the wonderful happenings of our many years together, the list grew almost endless. Consequently I decided to concentrate more on this list and less on the shorter one with the reasons for going.

Next I decided to be entirely honest and open with my husband. I told him I had been very unhappy recently and that I had been blaming all of my unhappiness on him and his drinking. Then I said I finally realized that he was not to blame for my unhappiness, that whether I was happy or not depended entirely on me and my attitude toward life. I admitted that I had been trying to change him into the person I wanted him to be, but finally realized I had many problems of my own which I should be working on instead.

Finally, I told him when I felt I couldn't control my anger and my criticism of him, I would leave the room and maybe go off to a movie or to visit friends. In addition, I planned to get involved in community activities so I could get my mind off of him and remember to concentrate on my own shortcomings.

My life began to take on new meaning as I learned that it didn't have to be centered around alcoholism and that I was becoming a person of value to my family, my friends, and the world around me.

Needless to say, there are still times when I get so frustrated I want to lash out and retaliate in any way I can for my hurts. However, as I expand my world, the number of occasions when my gestures of love and understanding are responded to in kind is increasing, and that has made a significant difference in my life.

Thank you, dear Heavenly Father, for giving me the courage to realize that I alone am responsible for my own happiness.

Gladys

27

A FATHER'S LOVE

When Christ taught His disciples to regard God as their Father in Heaven He did not mean that their idea of God must necessarily be based upon their ideas of their own fathers. . . It is the relationship that Christ is stressing. The intimate love for, and interest in, his son possessed by a good earthly father represents to men a relationship that they can understand, even if they themselves are fatherless!
J. B. Phillips

"I promise that if you are good . . ." That's how the promises from my alcoholic father all started, but no matter how good I was, they seldom came true. It is in the alcoholic nature to break promises, and it is in the nature of the child of an alcoholic to believe that the lack of fulfillment of the promises is his fault.

Small wonder, then, that when we have shed our childhood clothing and conduct, the lack of trust remains. Small wonder, too, the difficulty we have had with the concept of a "loving Father-God," who will perform on schedule, as promised, every time.

When I began to deal with the concept of a "Higher Power" rather than a Father-God, I felt a wave of guilt. I was sure that this was heretical, wrong, and another step on my road to Hell. I was to quickly find, however, that prayer works in the face of guilt. I prayed often to my new unseen Higher Power for forgiveness and for the strength to allow my concept of It to expand past the "heavenly critical parent" limitations that had previously given me trouble.

As my concept of God has expanded over time, I have seen many other limitations fall by the wayside. I have found that whatever limits I place on God are actually limits that I am placing on my own life. An unlimited God, Higher Power, Infinite Invisible, or whatever wording is most comfortable allows for an unlimited amount of good to be demonstrated in my life.

Thank You, Lord, for giving me unlimited blessings in spite of my limited vision.

Ed

I LOVE YOU DAD, REGARDLESS

This is the promise: that if you honor your father and mother, yours will be a long life, full of blessing.
Ephesians 6:3 (TLB)

I dearly loved my father. He was witty, loved his family, and was a joy to be with - when he was sober.

Dad was a staff photographer for the city newspaper. His hectic work schedule covering anything from social activities to murder and suicide took a heavy toll on his happy-go-lucky spirit. Our family also suffered because we couldn't depend on his coming home on a regular basis, or routinely providing for our financial needs.

One of the hardest things for me to bear as a teenager, was the embarrassment Dad caused us. We lived in a small suburb, and everyone knew everyone else's business. All my schoolmates knew my Dad, and when they saw me coming, I often heard them snicker "Her old man sure can't hold his booze."

Early in life I learned to pray, and I faithfully took my problems to God. I couldn't understand why He allowed my Dad to continue making such a fool of himself and his family, but I kept praying anyway. Dad never did quit drinking, although he promised over and over that he would. God did help me and our family, however, to learn to live with the problem, but it wasn't easy.

As I grew older, I found other young people in school had their share of family problems too. One had an alcoholic parent like mine; another had a brother in prison, and one girl's mother had left home with another man. I realized that the embarrassment of alcoholism in the family is only one of the many battles young folks have to face.

My understanding pastor helped me accept the fact that I would have to make my own personality attractive and competitive enough that others would know me as myself, not as the daughter of a drunkard. I worked hard at my schoolwork and volunteer activities to do that.

The inferiority complex that hindered me as a youngster was eventually beaten down by my determination to prove that even though my Dad was the victim of alcoholism, I was not going to go through life ashamed of him. I loved him too much for that, and I didn't care who knew it. But I also cared about myself enough to rise, with God's help, above the humiliation he caused me, and I know I am a more compassionate adult and parent because of what I've been through.

Dear Father, thank you for helping me remember Dad as a dear loving father, and for teaching me the meaning of compassion.

Georgia

BITTERNESS, RELUCTANCE, AND HEALING FORGIVENESS

Get rid of all bitterness, rage and anger, brawling and slander, along with every form of malice. Be kind and compassionate to one another, forgiving each other, just as in Christ God forgave you.
Ephesians 4:31-32 (NIV)

At first my husband's drinking caused deep heartache. But as time passed, other more hostile feelings took over. As the months turned into years, my anger changed into deep-seated bitterness until it was the only emotion I felt towards him.

My normal response, when mistreated, was to nurse the wrong and feed on its pain. But when I did that, when I allowed the wound to fester into hatred, it twisted my thought processes until I became an emotional slave to my alcoholic. The memory of past treatment was always just below the surface of my consciousness where it could consistently distort my response to his current actions. Consequently being around him was unbearable because I was bound, as if by chains, to all the pain of the past.

Though I knew I had to let go of my bitterness and forgive my husband, my initial reaction was, "Why should I? He doesn't deserve my forgiveness."

Much of my reluctance came because I thought by forgiving him I'd be condoning his behavior. But as I thought about how God forgives me, I began to see that forgiveness on His part didn't mean God approved of my behavior. When I did something wrong God didn't hold any resentment against me. He simply forgave me because He chose to. And I was to forgive others, not because they deserved my forgiveness, but because God had forgiven me.

When I finally chose to forgive my husband, the emotional chains of hatred dropped away. Forgiveness freed me to respond in a constructive way and I no longer reacted inappropriately to his negative behavior.

Forgiveness also helped to ease the pain of the past. I could look back on past heartaches and no longer feel the intensity of their pain.

But of all the things forgiveness did for me, one stands out above all the rest. Forgiveness freed me to love my husband once again.

Thank you, Lord, for your forgiveness and for helping me to see that I must forgive others, both for Your sake as well as my own.

Melanie

THE TERRIFYING TIME MACHINE

Not drunk is he who from the floor
Can rise alone and still drink more . . .
Thomas Love Peacock

As an independent drunk, I didn't cause my companions much trouble. I rarely threw up, seldom passed out, and could drink strong men under the table. Perhaps that is why it took me so long to realize I had a problem.

The most obvious symptom of my problem was a secret I shared with very few. From the onset of drunkenness to the morning after, I entered a time machine and went off into the land of no-memory. I seldom told this because I didn't think anyone would believe me. And if they did, I was sure they would think I was crazy because I was beginning to think so myself.

Countless alcoholics wander the streets and the bars carrying this same terrible secret, believing they are unique, possibly deranged. There is something so spooky, so terrifying, about blackouts.

Once I read of an alcoholic picked up on suspicion of murder. He couldn't supply an alibi because he didn't know where he had been. While I was never called on to supply an alibi, I was often called on to answer searching questions: Where have you been? What did you do with the money? Why is your dress torn?

No use saying, "I don't remember." They'd believe anything before they'd believe that. So I became a teller of elaborate tales, a consummate liar.

Physically, I probably would have been able to rise above the floor for a few more years, but what good is a functioning body without a brain to direct it? What good is the day when you can't remember the night?

When I finally sought help from Alcoholics Anonymous, I wept with relief to learn that alcoholism is an illness, and that one of its primary symptoms is the blackout. The program of recovery is made up of twelve steps, the second of which spoke directly to my problem: Came to believe that a Power greater than ourselves could restore us to sanity. So I was not wicked or crazy, and if I did as suggested I could hope to get well.

I can't pretend it was easy in the beginning, but there were new caring friends to help me, and a God who listened to my prayers. Now, years later, living without alcohol has become a beautiful way of life. And I always know where I was last night!

Thank you, dear God, for restoring me to sanity.

Nancy

TOUGH LOVE, THE BEGINNING

O God! that men should put an enemy in their mouths to steal away their brains.
William Shakespeare

My life and drinking were in control. I worked hard and needed relaxation at day's end. This didn't hurt me or my family, and I was a good mother. I even sent the kids to church on Sunday while I "rested."

Certainly I wasn't alcoholic - not me! Now Dad, he was an alcoholic. Lost his job, drank continually, and spent much time institutionalized. That was alcoholism. I just drank to relax, that's all.

Dinner hours grew later as the numbers of highballs I consumed increased, along with family complaints. Too "tired" to cook, I varied menus only with the selection of help available for hamburger in the supermarket. Relationships deteriorated.

One day my eighteen-year-old daughter confronted me with the truth about my drinking, forced me to look at myself as others saw me, and then she moved out! Devastated, I realized the horrible nightmare my life had become. I'd hit bottom, but a merciful God allowed a reasonably gentle fall. I'd been an alcoholic for so very long and didn't realize it. My daughter's tough love was my turning point because it made me face reality and gave me the courage to change.

My recent introduction to God's love at a nearby church prompted me to consult the pastor after she left, and with his help I began traveling down that road to recovery.

Today, my grandchildren at play remind me that many of my children's early years were stolen from my brain. But I'm so grateful for the good years we've had since my last drink which was the day after my daughter walked out - temporarily!

Father, thank you for giving me a wise and caring daughter who loved me enough to get tough.

Isabel

TOUGH LOVE, CHAPTER 2

Love seeks one thing only: the good of the one loved.
Thomas Merton

The child of an alcoholic, I too found solace in a bottle until my own brave daughter confronted me with reality, and then moved out until I could put my life in order. She provided the tough love that led me to sobriety. Now it was my turn to pass that on.

Dad's alcoholism created the usual horrendous problems for years. Long free from my own bondage, I felt tremendous compassion for his pathetic state, but that alone wasn't enough. He was being released from an institution following another attempt to get well, but he couldn't go home because my mother's health was too precarious for her to have to cope with him.

Since I operated an adult care facility, I tried to help Dad by offering him custodial care in my home - with one provision: if he created any problems with his behavior, he would have to leave immediately. For a few weeks following his release, during long pre-breakfast chats while I worked in the kitchen, we developed a closeness we'd not known previously.

Then one evening he went out, returning drunk, angry, and threatening a brawl. It was late, the other residents were asleep, and I knew his continued presence in that condition would undermine the security those elderly folks had come to expect. That left me with no choice but to call the police for help.

Was it the right thing to do? Yes. God didn't tell us life was going to be easy if we followed him, but He did say that He would be with us always and that includes the times when we have to make tough choices. It not only grieved me to evict my father, it also hurt to be treated by the authorities as some cold-hearted witch for leaving him homeless in the dead of winter. But giving in would help no one. I knew how violent he could become, and I could not expose the elderly folks in my home to that dangerous behavior.

The aftermath of this episode brought many months of sobriety for Dad, in his own home. Had I allowed him to manipulate me that cold winter night, I doubt he would have made the effort. Often we must make some seemingly cruel choices if we are to help our alcoholic. Like the daughter who made a tough choice for me, I had to make one for my dad despite the pain it caused me.

Lord, thank you for giving me the strength to make a tough love choice too.

Isabel

A STRANGE NEW FRIEND

*He hath sent me . . . to proclaim liberty to the captives, and the opening
of the prison to them that are bound.*
Isaiah 61:1 (KJV)

Sometimes the help that changes our lives comes from the strangest places.
God, who is Love, used love to free me from alcohol so that I could learn
to love Him too. All those years of drinking, of causing untold misery to
others and soul sickness to myself, led me to a place where I was all alone.
All my friends and family had given up on me.

And so it was I found myself in a strange new town with a strange new job,
and God sent me a strange new friend. She was supportive, but it was
obvious that she sorely disapproved of my drinking. My behavior grew
worse and worse in proportion to the extent that my self-esteem was
destroyed. Anyone who has been enslaved in the ravages of alcohol will
recognize what I'm speaking of. This special woman gave of herself over
and over again and, in spite of the way I continually "tested" her, she stuck
close and did not end our friendship.

One day, however, she talked to me specifically about the need to stop
drinking. She told me how much it hurt her and my children. Others had
tried to help before, but for some strange reason I listened to her. I vowed
to quit and turned over all my liquor bottles to her. My home was thoroughly
cleaned out!

It was hard, this quitting! But I would keep seeing her sweet face before
me, her eyes brimming with tears. And somehow, some way, with the help
of God, I made it day by day through that long but victorious summer.

Though I did not know God in any personal way at that time, He knew me.
He knew what would motivate me sufficiently to quit and He arranged my
life accordingly.

Now my relationship with my strange friend is only a wonderful memory.
Our paths parted not long after I stopped drinking. Bit by bit the Lord filled
the void she left in my life and His love for me has made all the difference.
Ten years later, I am still sober and I can say with conviction because I
understand what it means, He does indeed set the captives free!

Help me, O Lord, to always remember where You brought me from, and
what You are making of me.

Lynda

THE EXECUTIVE ALCOHOLIC

...divine strength is not usually given us until we are fully aware of our weakness

Thomas Merton

I understood the truth of the paradox Merton speaks of after I took a trip to hell and back. Two laws of the culture I came from guided me there: (1) A winner always focuses on his strengths but never on his weaknesses, and (2) A man must drink but never is a drunkard.

These laws served me well at first. At age 37 I became an executive in a large corporation. A sense of strength and power filled me. There was no doubt I was a man; I could hold my liquor. And booze fueled my power. Whenever I had feelings of fear or insecurity, booze transformed those feelings into courage and confidence.

A few years later, something went wrong. Booze no longer transformed me; instead, it enslaved me. I drank more just to function and couldn't stop no matter what I tried. My mornings were nightmares of remorse and horror. I was unemployed, alcohol had landed me in jail, and I was threatened with divorce. I also figured I was on God's blacklist. I'd prayed that if He'd get me out of these problems, I'd stop drinking, but He hadn't. Subconsciously I was terrified, while consciously I clung to my two old laws. Tomorrow I would be strong enough. Always tomorrow.

Then one morning my daughter said, "Daddy, did you know you vomited all over the table at dinner last night?" No, I did not know. But the revolting scene I could imagine sickened me. It also shocked me into being honest with myself, and I decided to seek help. That same day a friend guided me to a fellowship of alcoholics who knew how to get sober and stay sober, and that was the beginning of my 12 sober years of life to date.

That bunch of former sots said they'd found that Divine strength was the only thing which could conquer their addiction. They'd prayed like I had, bargaining with God, but that hadn't worked. What had worked was to trust God, acknowledge their weaknesses, and work hard to lose the laws of their old lives - including those two laws I was sure my life depended on. A painful pill, but I decided to try their crazy scheme and it brought me back from hell.

God's Grace - and once you have experienced it there is no other word for it, - has given me a new life of dignity, freedom and wholeness which is an incredible replacement for that "manly" self-centered executive life I once had.

Thank you, Dear Lord, for all the manifestations of that wonderful, intangible, reality known as your "Grace."

Vic

PLAINTIVE PETITIONS -
POSITIVE PRAYERS

It's one thing to tell God that you hurt and quite another thing to go on and on vividly describing your pain. If you ask God to help you pray positively, He will gradually turn your optimism and prayers toward positive thoughts about the future.
Andre Bustanoby

One or both of us had laid awake night after night, week after week, month after month, waiting for the sound of our daughter's car. One Saturday night she didn't come home at all. The next day friends delivered her to our doorstep because she was so drunk she couldn't walk. Still another night the police, with all their lights flashing, brought her home because she was driving erratically down a heavily trafficked, treacherous hill.

In the mornings my wife and I would automatically inspect her car for new dents, broken lights, smashed doors. Through we spoke to her in the evenings about the danger of her behavior, we got nowhere.

At last we faced up to our helplessness and turned the matter over to God. Or maybe I should say we tried to because there were a lot of times when we weren't convinced He was doing a good job so we took the responsibility back. Then we would pray all the more earnestly, not to instruct God, but to remind ourselves that only in God could we have hope. That helped, and eventually we found the courage to stop the lecturing, eliminate the yelling, and go to sleep at night.

To others our prayer life might have resembled a game of tug-of-war with God, but perhaps it was nothing more than our learning to replace negative prayers with positive ones. But regardless of how you describe those petitions, it wasn't until after we changed our patterns that our daughter reached a turning point herself.

It came because she couldn't remember what she had done the night before and that scared her into sobriety. She couldn't do it alone, but with the help of AA she found once more the control she had lost.

Still we were skeptical, so we kept placing her into the care of God. But as the days of her sobriety became weeks and then months, our hope began to rise. We finally realized our prayers had been answered the night she came directly home from an AA meeting, flung herself into an easy chair as she had done years before, and asked, "What are you guys doing tonight?" Then we knew our daughter wanted to be a part of our lives again and was ours once more.

Thank you, Father, for the healing of our daughter and the evidence of your spirit moving through our lives.

Rolland

SUCH PAIN,
SUCH EXTRAORDINARY PAIN

I had been unable to rescue myself from my own living death until I finally learned to say the three most difficult words - I need help!
Lillian Roth

I believed that "death was the only answer." As I sat with the bottle to my mouth looking at the pills in my hand, I remembered how my alcoholic father had spoken those same words so many years before. I respected him for his sensitivity; I admired him for his courage; and I believed in his way of thinking. Death was his message. He thought it was the answer to his problems, but my father lived on in pain, such extraordinary pain.

Quickly I put the pills in my mouth, then washed them down with the liquor and sat waiting to die. I respected myself for my sensitivity; I admired my courage; and I believed in my way of thinking. Death was the answer I thought, but I lived on in pain, such extraordinary pain.

My life was unbearable and my thoughts were confusing, but I didn't know where to turn. Though I addressed "God" when asking for help, I didn't know Him and I couldn't feel His presence. Throughout that period of my life, God chose to use people as instruments for His peace, but despite the fact that I was momentarily touched by each of those messengers, the bottle continued to call me. I resented my sensitivity. I'd lost my courage, and I hated my way of thinking. Despite my attempts to die, I lived on in pain, such extraordinary pain.

Several years and many messages later, God touched my innermost being by creating in me a desire for help; a desire for hope. When I felt desperate I remembered that I had been given a phone number of a member of Alcoholics Anonymous. A year later I finally called that number and reached out for help even though I thought I just wanted to die. Life seemed too much to bear.

The woman I contacted gave me love that she said she had been given. Though I wasn't sure what she meant, she seemed to care. An image of God appeared within me in the form of the feeling of love. God was in my heart before I even knew He existed. He replaced my weakness with humility and laid before me a pathway to eternal life. He let me know He respected my sensitivity. He refilled me with courage, and He gave me a new way of thinking. Life was His message and I lived on in peace, such extraordinary peace.

Thank you, God, for believing in me when I was unable to believe in myself.

Margaret

MY GREATEST MISTAKE

Unless life is lived for others, it is not worthwhile.
Mother Teresa

Some people say that my greatest mistake was to marry a man with a serious drinking problem.

Other people, more enlightened perhaps, point out that my greatest mistake, especially in the early part of my marriage, was my failure to relinquish my husband to God. I should have learned to "stop trying," they said and "start trusting."

The second group was closer to making an accurate observation than the first, I think. But neither was exactly on target. For I now find that my greatest mistake was that I stopped being a giver.

There was something about the continual upheaval of our home that rendered me insecure and anxious and very self-absorbed. As my husband drank us deeper into debt, I no longer felt we could afford to give to other people who were in need. I also began to believe that I carried such a heavy emotional load that I could no longer bear to take an in-depth interest in other people and their problems.

As the wife of an alcoholic, I became almost totally focused on my chaotic home life and my worries. I was obsessed with finding solutions, I told myself. But in reality I was obsessed with me. That's a hard thing to admit to oneself, but I thank God for the insight, for it has changed my life.

It has taken me many years and countless struggles to grasp the truth that the essence of life is living for and giving to other people. If I had those early years of marriage to live over, I would give a lot more affection and concern to my husband. And if he rebuffed me, I would give of my time and energy to others in need.

Giving to others is its own reward. If I had made it a habit to be aware of others' needs and to try to meet them, I would have increased my ability to trust God, for I have discovered that when we meet others' needs, He takes care of us; even when we have an alcoholic spouse.

Dear Lord, please help me to entrust my needs to You so that I may be free to meet the needs of others.

Karen

I COULDN'T EVEN DIE RIGHT!

And I was with you in weakness, and in fear, and in much trembling.
I Corinthians 2:3 (KJV)

I am an alcoholic, and during the twenty-four years I drank I tried to commit suicide several times. When I look back at that time I'm amazed I'm still alive. Then I hated the world, but most of all I hated myself. And because I felt so totally worthless, I found it impossible to believe that anyone could love me.

To compensate I drank on a daily basis and made sure that no one knew the amount of alcohol I was consuming. Although I knew I had a very serious problem and I was lonesome and scared, I found it impossible to talk to anyone about it.

Eventually I stopped trying to pretend and I just drank. I consciously tried to drink myself to death because I couldn't live with the things I had done. I had been married and divorced seven times, and I couldn't work because I couldn't concentrate - I really thought I was losing my mind. The blackouts were getting longer and longer and I was never sure where or when I would wake up.

One of my worst memories is waking up at my sister's house and literally crawling to the bathroom. By the time I finished vomiting, I couldn't move. As I lay there on the bathroom floor, my niece came in crying and said, "Aunt Diane, are you going to die? Please don't. I love you."

"Not again," I thought. "I can't stand this any longer. God help me." I've since realized that God did help me when He sent my niece into that bathroom, that He was with me in my weakness and in my fear.

A few days later I decided to go into a treatment program and began attending AA. When I walked into that first meeting I felt like I had come home. I cried from sheer joy that at last I had found someone like me. All I had to do was say, "Hi. I'm Diane and I'm an alcoholic." They understood and accepted me as I was.

I hate to say that I drank again, but I did. Since I couldn't yet deal with the past and didn't know how to deal with the present, I used the old standby booze to take away the hurt. However, this time I immediately went into a treatment center where I finally began to learn about living without alcohol.

Today, after nineteen months of sobriety, I look forward to each day. I've learned that I can't change the past, but with God's help I can make today something worth remembering.

Thank you for each day of sobriety, Dear God.

Diane

AN OASIS OF LIGHT

The people who walked in darkness have seen a great light.
Isaiah 9:2 (RSV)

"Hey, God! How 'bout helping my Dad?" That was my childhood prayer. It was a prayer God heard, understood and answered, but you couldn't tell me that then. To me, it looked like God had no place in His world for my father, or that He heard my prayers for him.

When I passed early childhood and began to question my faith I came to the sudden and final decision that God was Bunk! I could see no place that my faith had worked for me. My dad was still drunk and my life was still filled with fear, insecurity, and pain. The only pay-off for faith that I could see was in some later life called Heaven and I didn't know of anyone who had been there and back. Therefore I reasoned, it was all another con-job by a minister.

And so I went about my life without worrying about God and what He thought about me, and I discovered it is a lot easier to stay drunk when you've pushed God out of your life. And that's where I kept Him for twenty-three years. Not only was my lack of faith convenient and expedient, it provided another reason for staying drunk.

Then for some unknown reason I began to feel a vague spiritual longing, that you might call a sense of, or a lack of fulfillment. The amount I drank seemed to make no difference, except perhaps, to make the feeling grow. God seemed to have found me on my barstool, and I wanted Him to leave me alone, or take me away from it for good.

My need to come to grips with God finally led me to a place where I would try to pray the prayers of my childhood, this time for me. And the words brought back the anger, the frustration, and the hatred of a God who had failed me. I screamed curses at Him from the bottomless well of my sickness. On the way to take my own life, I shouted shameful, unprintable accusations at him in my loudest voice, and ended with an anguished cry for help.

In the cold, motionless black hole which surrounded me and filled my soul, a small light, dim and distant, appeared. I felt it more than saw it. An oasis of light in the "dark night of the soul." That was all it was, but that was all it took.

Over the years that light has grown through the love and caring of those like me in recovery. It is the light that we see in each others' eyes as we share experiences, strength, and hope. It is the light I now see in my Father's eyes after all these years.

Lord, thank you for answering my prayer with a beautiful beginning when I wanted to end it all.

Ed

THERE'S NOTHING WRONG WITH ME!

Condemnation does not liberate, it oppresses.
                        C. G. Jung

I didn't know if I belonged. At Al-Anon, a support group for families and friends of alcoholics, I felt sorry for the people who had absorbed years of verbal abuse. Some lacked self-esteem, while others in the group were cynical or wallowed in the mire of self-pity.

I wasn't that way. Of course, the more I talked about my problems the more I seemed to embellish the facts so my friends would understand my misery. For some reason I took real pleasure in imagining them saying later, "My isn't she brave carrying on so well under such a terrible burden." But there's nothing wrong with me!

Some at Al-Anon cried out in anger and frustration. "At least I'm not like that," I said, not knowing my self-righteousness was showing.

My husband drank too much. The clink of ice in a glass signified it was 5:00 p.m. At 5:15 he would "freshen" it. By 5:30 he was ready for dinner. When I misjudged the time and he had to wait for dinner, I chuckled to myself. Sometimes I enjoyed throwing off his schedule and fixed dinner a few minutes early. I was playing a silly game.

He's the one with the problem, right? Every morning after he left for work, I checked the mark I put on the bottle and figured out how much he drank the night before. But there was nothing wrong with me!

When I learned about "detaching" and that I shouldn't rely on another person for my happiness, I became so involved with myself and my interests that I lost track of my husband's likes, dislikes and needs. We became roommates. My husband had a drinking problem and melodramatically I said that I loved him too much to sit and watch him kill himself. What did I want? I wanted out. But there was nothing wrong with me!

Then I met a Pastor who said I could find God's answer for my life in Bible study. Following his advice I threw myself into studying because I really needed to know yesterday what I should be doing today. I didn't find the answer immediately; it took a lot of reading and reflective thought before I realized there was something wrong with me: I had a terrible attitude. No, I couldn't change my husband; he had to do that himself. But I could change the way I responded to him, and I could work at healing our relationship, and the Bible contained the help I needed to do that.

Thank you, Lord, for helping me to see that I have a problem too, and that I am the only one who can solve it.

                        Louise

WHEN WORK IS A GIFT

Work is not primarily a thing one does to live, but the thing one lives to do. It is, or should be, the full expression of the worker's faculties, the thing in which he finds spiritual, mental and bodily satisfaction, and the medium in which he offers himself to God.
Dorothy L. Sayers

I was a good secretary. In fact, my skills were above average in the beginning. In a few short years, however, everything changed, for I became an alcoholic.

How strange, the disease of alcoholism. There was a time when, as a result of those few morning drinks, the only difficulty I had was occasional confusion as I did the filing. But one day, as I was taking dictation, I noticed my hand trembling. The lines and curves of my shorthand figures began to take on strange, unfamiliar shapes.

As the shaking of my hands increased, so did the number of my typing errors. My electric typewriter was unmerciful. Each time a trembling finger touched the wrong key, that key leaped to the paper, gleefully scrambling the letters.

At first I denied the problem. "I'm just a little nervous," I said, excusing myself.

When I fell behind in my work, I began putting in overtime, sitting alone in the office and using two fingers to hunt-and-peck my way through a pile of correspondence. But then the day came when I was forced to surrender to my illness.

Thanks to God and Alcoholics Anonymous I did recover and I'll never forget the day I returned to work. A new office; a new beginning! How proud I felt facing an electric keyboard once again and snapping my way sharply through a stack of mail. Never before had I fully appreciated what a blessing it is to be able to work.

Today the ringing of my alarm clock is the signal for me to slip out of bed, to my knees, and offer a prayer of thanksgiving for the miraculous gift of a productive job and the ability to do it well.

Let me work for your glory this day, Lord God.

Doris

JUST AS HE IS RIGHT NOW

Judge not . . . condemn not. . .
Luke 6:37 (RSV)

Just because you make up your mind, once and for all, to stand by your alcoholic spouse regardless of the heartaches you suffer, doesn't mean it's going to be easy. The frustration and the anger will still persist in popping their ugly little heads right through your best intentions even during a constant stream of positive healing affirmations and prayers. I know, because I've been there.

Like countless others, I reminded myself again and again that when I agreed to stay I knew there were going to be mountains to climb. Still the broken promises, the uncalled for bursts of temper, and the dreadfully embarrassing episodes haven't been easy to take.

Sometimes I have been overpowered by the hate and the resentment I've felt for my spouse. At times like that when I've asked, "How can you go on living with those awful feelings?" I've been told, "You must release in love." And when that didn't work, "If you can't release in love, release any way you can." But how can you release something that has such a strong hold on you and your entire existence?

One morning I got out of bed and stood looking down upon him as he lay heavily inhaling and exhaling. Each breath still reeked of an accidental "slip" the night before. I felt the now familiar anger and resentment growing within me and decided I simply could not tolerate this feeling any longer. "Dear God," I begged, "let me accept him exactly as he is right now - without condemnation and without judgment. Then let me release him to find his own pathway to peace in mind and in body." Relief washed over me as soon as I finished that prayer and I quickly wrote down the words so I wouldn't forget them.

I came to the decision that it was not, and it never could be, within my power to change this man I still loved despite the anguish his disease had caused me. And I knew that even though we might never have a healthy relationship, our relationship could be free of my hate and anger, if I would accept him exactly as he was at the moment, and exactly as he would be as he went about making his own changes.

From then on, every time I felt resentment welling up inside of me I repeated my spontaneous prayer. Sometimes I still have to say it ten or twenty times a day, but always I feel peace and relief as I do so.

Thank you, Dear God, for helping me realize that I had to choose between nursing resentment and the soothing balm of release and acceptance.

Gladys

THE FEAR OF ABANDONMENT

And every fear limits our expectations.
                    Paula D'Arcy

You're going to be a father! I met the announcement of my wife's pregnancy with the normal rush of pride, the usual masculine emotional swagger, and the traditional pang of fear that accompanies such news. And then, I thought about it. A baby would focus my wife's attention away from me and I would be forced to do for myself and the family; trapped into a job; sentenced to be a good example; condemned to a life of dirty-diaper boredom. Even worse, I would be part of, not all of.

The coming event left me feeling frightened. Growing up in an alcoholic home, I had come to believe that the world was my fault, my responsibility, and mine to manage. The only salvation from this burden was the total attentiveness and love of someone outside of me. Second place was no place at all, and a baby would put me in second place. When I got to that point in my thinking, I experienced a great fear of abandonment.

My response was to binge throughout the pregnancy, blaming the binges on happiness over my coming fatherhood. The day the baby was born, I celebrated her arrival with an increased dose of my self-pity medicine. And that's the way it was through two marriages and three children.

As the children grew, I would withdraw even more for protection of my fragile ego. Each child became a competitor in my life. I competed for the love of their mothers and lost every battle. The addiction increased with each loss and the loneliness within my own families became unbearable. When it did, I walked away just like my father had.

It took many years experiencing the love of the AA program for me to see this abandonment of my families for what it was, and even longer for me to see my father's abandonment of his children and wife was exactly the same. When the fear of abandonment grew beyond our ability to deal with it, we left before they did so that we could still feel in control of our lives. Now I know that both physical and emotional abandonment are classic responses to irrational fears but all I knew then was that I had to run, to get out.

What I know now is that my fears will not drive the God I know away. He has never abandoned me. Nor will my projections cause His love to falter. And, through that love, I am able to heal my wounds and those that I have caused.

Today, Lord, let me know again that Your love is forever and ever.

                    Ed

THE ONLY PEACE I KNOW

Peace I leave with you; my peace I give you. I do not give to you as the world gives.

John 14:27 (NIV)

I live in a home where frustration reigns supreme because I never know what to expect. Is my father going to be funny, silly and sweet, or is he going to be angry, mean and sarcastic? The fear keeps me tense, nervous, silent and I pretend that all is well so people can't discover my secret.

No matter how hard I try, something always seems to set him off and he attacks my hair, my clothes, my personality, my friends, my grades or whatever. With every drunken word he shatters my self-esteem. He won't remember in the morning what he said, but I will. I don't dare show the hurt though because it will give him more ammunition. Sound like a battle? You bet it is and I'm just trying to survive.

How I long for release from this prison that is my home. My mother, forever scarred from the affects of alcoholism, can never be a real mother to me. My father's mother raises me, covering up for my father all along the way. If I could have just one day where I wasn't worried, frightened, ashamed and grown-up, well, I can't really imagine what it would be like, but I'd like to.

It seems as though this misery will last forever. At times, when he hasn't had a drink for a day or two, my hope is renewed, and I try to be the best daughter I can so he won't feel the need to drink again. It seems to be working and then one night he doesn't come home until very late and my hope is dashed to pieces.

The truth is I have no control over anything. No one knows this because I'm friendly and always laughing, hiding my pain to all but one.

Someone told me about God. I don't know who, when, where or how. All I know is that He is my only Friend - the only one who knows my secret. Somehow, I am comforted even though the nightmare rages on day after day after day. My friendship with God is the only peace I know.

Deep inside my heart there is an assurance that there is a plan and purpose for my life beyond this present pain. I feel that no matter what, I will survive this. Not just survive, but fully live.

Thank you, Lord, that in the midst of anguish and despair, You give me peace and hope.

Lezlie

I'LL NEVER HAVE FUN ANYMORE!

What contemptible scoundrel stole the cork from my lunch?
W. C. Fields

Probably more funny lines about intoxication are attributed to W. C. Fields than to anyone else. But to those who live in the nether world of chronic drunkenness, there's not much to laugh about. Somewhere along the line friends stop saying, "You were so funny last night," and the alcoholic meets cold stares of disapproval instead. He's no longer the life of the party; he's just a pain in the neck.

Oh, yes, most of us had fun in the beginning. Booze removed our inhibitions, and we could be very funny. But with the passage of time it took more and more alcohol to bring on that great euphoria. We crossed over the invisible line between social drinking and alcoholism, and booze failed to do for us what it once did. Instead, it took us into a shadowy world where there was no laughter and no fun, but we returned to that world again and again in a desperate attempt to recapture the magic.

The turning point for me came one terrible morning when I climbed the stairs leading to an Alcoholics Anonymous club room because I couldn't live with what my life had become any longer. Panting and sweating, I found myself thinking, *"If I stop drinking, I'll never have fun anymore,"* totally forgetting that I hadn't had any fun in a long time. But at the top of those stairs I found bright-eyed, laughing people. Were they crazy? Not by a long shot! Through the spiritual program of AA, they had found what I had been looking for in the bottle - peace, serenity, and the joy of living.

One lady was wearing a pin that read, *"Reality is for people who can't handle booze."* While I thought that was funny, I also knew it was true.

After several months of precarious sobriety, I entered into the fun. I bought a Jack Daniel's T-shirt, which I often wore when lunching with friends who enjoyed a glass of the bubbly. And I found a bumper sticker which read SOBER AND CRAZY. When urged to have a drink by people who knew nothing of my past, I learned to airily say, "I don't drink - but I do everything else." (It wasn't true, but it always got a laugh.)

Today, after years of sobriety, I'm grateful that I am an alcoholic. The program of Alcoholics Anonymous taught me to face life and enjoy it without artificial stimulation, but best of all, it brought me closer to the God of my understanding.

Thank you, Lord, for leading me up that flight of stairs when there was nowhere else to go but down.

Nancy

DRY MEANS TOTALLY, COMPLETELY DRY

Like a city whose walls are broken down is a man who lacks self-control.
Proverbs 25:28 (NIV)

Perhaps there is no lonelier person than a single alcoholic. At least it seems that way to me because for years my alcoholism and my loneliness compounded each other.

When I became a Christian I thought my alcohol problems were solved forever and didn't realize the illness had simply moved off stage, waiting for the excitement of my new life to wear thin. And there it waited in the wings for almost five years.

Then suddenly I was alone again. No longer surrounded by a fellowship of friends who valued their relationship with God, that old demon alcoholism didn't waste any time in seeking center stage. "Hey," he said, "you don't have to get wasted like you used to - just tip a few beers and help yourself make it through this hard time."

What could it hurt, I foolishly reasoned with him. After all, I am a new person, and I have much more self control than before. I'll never get as bad as I was. But I did. In less than three months I was hooked again, out of control and my faith-centered life was in a tail-spin.

Then I started dating a wonderful woman who eventually became my wife even though I almost lost her the day she found beer in my refrigerator. Surely it must have been God's guidance that kept her from walking out of my life because she certainly wasn't convinced by the flimsy excuse I gave for why it was there.

One day she called me when I was half drunk and I couldn't make my words come out right so I made an excuse to hang up. Then, thoroughly shaken by the lie I'd told, I dissolved into tears and felt the Spirit of God directing my thoughts and forcing me to take a long, hard look at what I was doing to my own life. Here was a beautiful, faith-filled woman who was serious about our relationship and I was choosing booze instead of her.

I didn't want to lose her, so I stopped drinking that day and never had another drop. A few months later we were married and today, after years of happy, permanent sobriety, I have, truly and permanently, recovered. Now I know that I can never, ever, for any reason take even a single drop. The demon no longer has a role to play in my life for I'm dry, totally dry, and I plan to stay that way forever.

Thank you Lord, for loving me enough to show me the way out.

Kevin

SANDY'S STORY

Endure and persist; this pain will turn to your good by and by.
                                        Ovid

Will and I had a great time in the early years of our marriage. Impromptu get-togethers were our specialty, but we never missed a party or a Saturday night on the town either.

Then suddenly I lost my desire to party, and that made our lifestyle seem ugly in my eyes. When I quit going out all the time, I was surprised to find that my teenage children were angry with me for staying home because I was robbing them of their freedom. And my husband was angry with me for not going with him, so he went by himself.

My daughter stopped talking to me and instead wrote notes that grew progressively more angry, while my son stayed in his room most of the time, beating on his practice pad or his dresser with his drumsticks. Will stopped speaking to me except when absolutely necessary, and he took off his wedding band. He rarely came home for meals any more. In fact, he rarely came home. The heartbreaker was the day he left a card on the table for my birthday; it was a get well card.

Eventually he moved out and a bittersweet peace settled into our home. Our nerves settled down and the children and I no longer stared at his empty place at the table, wondering what would happen when he did return. For a while the three of us clung together for support, and then it was back to work for me. The bills had to be paid. They were so relieved the tension was gone that they never noticed we ate out of the tomato patch a good part of the summer.

Many nights were spent with my head on a tear-soaked pillow. I sorely missed the husband I'd loved so dearly, but his drunken phone calls were no enticement to invite him back. As the months passed, the love I felt for him eventually turned to emptiness.

Then one day he called upon the name of the Lord for help, and never desired another drink. This frightened me as I wasn't sure it was real and I was afraid to believe him. It took a year and a half of persistent testing on my part and patience on his, before my answer turned from "No" to, "YES . . . come home." At that point I had to ask God to give me His love for my husband, to fill that empty void, and He did.

Today Will and I have a more beautiful and satisfying relationship than our early married life ever offered because our new life is built on a mutual respect that has helped us grow together.

Thank you, God, for helping me know when endurance and persistence were called for to rebuild our lives together.

                                        Sandy

WILL'S STORY

And I will restore to you the years that the locust hath eaten. . .
Joel 2:25 (KJV)

On a drive through western Pennsylvania I witnessed the destruction wrought by a recent tornado. Homes were destroyed, barns lay in shambles, and cement block buildings vanished. Jagged shafts, twisted and splintered, were all that remained of previously wooded areas. Lives had been lost, and material goods scattered to the winds, never to be recovered. Not so very different from an alcoholic's life, I reflected; my own being a prime example.

I worked hard at what I did. There was nothing so important as keeping my elbows on that bar. My "friends" were like-minded; promises, commitments, appointments, all dissolved like rainbows on the horizon. And, like the tornado, everywhere my life touched down, there was destruction.

I was so caught up in the whirlwind of partying, bars and "fun" that it came as a surprise when I couldn't stop the momentum. Nor did I want to, though the cost was great. My family was destroyed by the divorce brought on by my drinking, my parents painfully injured, any equity for the future negated, and my career development was severely hampered.

A second marriage and a second family later was history repeating itself. I couldn't live with them and I couldn't live without them. Finally we were all so miserable that I moved out, only to continually badger my wife Sandy about moving back. It wasn't until I realized that her firm "NO" really meant "NO" that I gradually came to see that I was beyond help.

It was at that point, when I came to the absolute end of myself, that I sought God in total desperation. "I need your help, God," I cried, "I can't do it myself."

God heard my prayer and began to show me the way out of that hell-bent rut. Step-by-step I followed His lead until at last I found my feet planted on solid ground. From that day to this, I haven't wanted a drop of the poison with which I tried to destroy myself.

Reconciliation and healing eventually followed my commitment and I awaken each day - even sixteen years later - grateful to be free of the guilt and the pain. And so very grateful for parents who prayed and for my wife Sandy who said "No" initially and waited to be sure my recovery was real before eventually saying "YES . . . come home."

Thank you, Lord, for setting me free, for Sandy's persistence, and for restoring our lives.

Will

THE HIDDEN VALUE OF PROBLEMS

Problems call forth our courage and our wisdom; indeed, they create our courage and our wisdom. It is only because of problems that we grow mentally and spiritually.
M. Scott Peck, M.D.

After my father died my mother came to live in an apartment built on the back of our house. While I knew that both my parents imbibed now and then, I was totally unaware to what extent my mother's drinking controlled her life.

From the time mom arrived we never had a day free from the nightmare of worry, anger and frustration. I never knew what escapade of my mother's my wife would report on my return from work each evening.

Her continual lying and denials were a constant source of friction between her and us and between my wife and me, thwarting all efforts for my mother to receive the help she needed.

My wife and I were new Christians when this all began and my mother's behavior drove us to our knees, searching for a solution. At one point my wife even considered leaving me because of the many problems engendered by the situation, and I wouldn't have blamed her.

What could have become a family tragedy became a triumph instead. Our marriage survived and in time my mother stopped drinking. What turned our lives around? We believe the source of those changes was prayer. Not an occasional "Help me, Lord" when we were feeling desperate, but an on-going honest dialogue with God asking Him to help us understand and deal with the problems we were facing. Because of our continually seeking God we both grew in spiritual stature much more readily than if we hadn't had this problem to contend with, and in time we actually became thankful for it.

God in His infinite wisdom and timing used a gall bladder attack and subsequent surgery to deliver us all from the whole nasty mess. On returning from the operating room, probably while she was still under the influence of the anesthetic, mother had what she termed a vision. As she later explained, the Lord visited her and told her many things resulting in her losing all desire for alcohol.

That happened over 20 years ago and she is still free. While mom was healed spiritually, she still suffers in her body from those flagrant violations, but all of us feel that is a small price to pay for her receiving eternal life and we praise God for the trials that caused us to grow.

Thank you, Father, for finding a way to reach my mother when all our earthly efforts failed.

Floyd

WARNING:
ALCOHOLISM CAN LEAD TO DEATH

Unquestionably, alcoholism is a terminal illness if untreated; yet, as the medical profession is slowly coming to realize, it is among the most treatable of all serious illnesses.
Jack B. Weiner

I just sort of hung around - and watched. The doctor said there was nothing more I could do.

The heart attack came first; then the personality change. And both the drinking and smoking intensified. "If your husband doesn't change his life style," the doctor said, "he'll die soon." But he also assured me that if he would quit smoking and reduce his alcohol intake, he could live a full productive life for many more years.

I watched him refuse change and thought, "This man is nuts!"

His was a different kind of terminal illness. It was the result of too many beers, too many scotch and waters, and too many inherited factors that indicated his alcoholism was a family disease for which he was not willing to seek or accept help.

He began to die a little at a time, day by day as his depression overpowered his ability and will to survive. It wasn't easy to watch, but I was addicted to him just as he was addicted to alcohol. In the end, after years of futile attempts to help him, all I could do was pray for the courage to stay with him while he acted out his death scenes on the stage of self-destruction. When the final curtain came down, I was glad I hadn't left.

The doctor had been right when he told me there was nothing more I could do. To put it another way, he might have said that we have no control over another's recovery or refusal of help, and I needed to know that alcoholism is a predictable, irreversible, progressive, and destructive disease that would kill my husband if he didn't quit drinking.

Thank you, God, for the warning that helped me deal with reality.

Barbara

MY PATH TO PEACEFULNESS

He restoreth my soul: he leadeth me in the paths of righteousness for his name's sake.
                              Psalms 23:3 (KJV)

Once I told a marriage counsellor that I would do anything to save my marriage, except to stop drinking. At that time my alcoholism had affected my thinking processes and I really believed that I would die if I didn't drink.

Then one day, after I sobered up from a binge, my wife sat me down, took my hand and said, "Paul, I love you, but I cannot continue to live with you if you continue to drink." I told her I would stop drinking and I meant it. But I meant it as a "temporary stopping."

As long as I believed I could drink again "when it all blew over" I could do it. During the next three months my brain cleared enough for me to respond to the little nudges God was giving me.

Encouraging me to get out and walk was one of the things He nudged me into doing. Almost before I knew what was happening, I was walking two miles every day on my lunch hour. One day, as I hiked along, I became aware of a wonderful sense of peacefulness and tranquility. I could hear crickets and birds; I saw the green grass and blue sky, and I felt "safe" for the first time since I was a kid.

There on that path I sensed a "presence" and I spoke to it out loud; "God if You are this peace, I surrender to You. Take me Lord."

Instantly I was flooded with an emotional release. I felt free, relieved of a burden, and filled with joy. Tears were running down my cheeks as I ran and jumped up and down, hollering at the top of my lungs, "I'm free, I'm free. Thank you, Lord, thank you, Lord." Anyone passing by might have thought I was crazy, but there was no one around for I was alone with my God.

When I finally did calm down I realized that the path I was on could symbolize the path of my life. It was all laid out for me. All I had to do was trust God and walk my path each day as I found it. I knew that he had laid that path out for me before I was born and that He would give me just what I needed to stay on it.

I have followed that path for several years now and it has led me to AA, Alcoholics for Christ, and sobriety. Now I say this prayer each day when I wake up:

Lord, please lead me on my path today at just the pace that's best for me.

                              Paul

MY MAGIC WORD

Train up a child in the way he should go, and when he is old he will not depart from it.
Proverbs 22:6 (RSV)

It's amazing what a difference one word can make in helping you cope with an on-going problem like alcoholism. For me that magic word is "detachment."

Like most parents I had the impression that good folks have good children. They don't drop out of school, have car wrecks, or write hot checks.

I thought I was one of those good parents until our son reached sixteen and I found he was addicted to alcohol. Then I began to question myself as I thought of everything I had done wrong in raising him. Guilt and fear became my constant companions as I wrestled with the past and dealt with the future by continually asking myself, "How can I help him?"

Eventually that question drove me to a parents group where a counsellor told me, "You didn't do it."

That lesson was reinforced when I heard a minister say, "God didn't blame Adam and Eve when Cain killed Abel." He gave our children free wills and good or bad, they are responsible for their choices.

The parent's group also helped me understand that my son is dealing with a disease. I didn't cause his alcoholism; I can't cure it, and try as I may, I cannot control it. What I can do is detach myself from the disease, but not the person. That doesn't mean that I have stopped caring; it means I've accepted the fact I can't deal with my son's addiction for him; he has to do it himself.

When I "detached" myself, I felt as though I stepped from darkness into daylight. What's more, I found I could sleep nights again too.

To be honest, the situation is still painful for me at times, especially when friends gloat over their good children's accomplishments, but I have learned to feel compassion instead of resentment for my son because I know the outcome of his life is not in my hands.

Help me, Father, not to be jealous of good children, but to thank you for my son, trusting that You will guide me to accept what I cannot change and to change whatever I can.

Lee

JUST ANOTHER LABEL

The intoxication of anger, like that of the grape, shows us to others, but hides us from ourselves.
Charles Caleb Colton

My dad has been an alcoholic for more than fifty years. I grew up with his constant drinking, not fully comprehending the whats and whys of alcoholism.

He has always been the type of man to live by one guideline: Smile and the world smiles with you, cry, and you cry alone. Dad basically followed those guidelines until my mother died, then he just gave up trying.

Despite the problems his drinking created I still loved him and that love brought my husband and myself, along with Dad's pastor, to put Dad through a chemical treatment program. Unfortunately, dad's sobriety only lasted two months.

I couldn't understand why his need to drink was more important than his family, nor could I cope with my wildly-fluctuating feelings about him. Like a pendulum, my emotions swung from loving him to hating him for depriving my children of the joys of having a grandpa.

Then one day I overheard my four-year-old son tell a friend that he loved Grandpa John, but his Mommy never lets him go to see him. When I heard that I first sat down and cried and then I proceeded to do a lot of soul searching.

Eventually it dawned on me that I wasn't protecting my boys, I was using that reason as an excuse to hide behind my own anger. After many sleepless nights I finally put things into proper prospective. If I had a friend who found out he had an incurable disease, I would not turn my back on him. On his bad days I would not put him down; I would reach out to hold his hand.

As often as I had heard the phrase "disease" I never believed alcoholism fit that category. To me it was just another label for people who wouldn't stop drinking.

Now I feel otherwise. My soul searching helped me see that Dad is the friend I would reach out to help, and alcoholism is his disease. I love my father and I try to tell him that when he calls or when we see each other. Sometimes he is sober, most of the time he is not. But no matter what, I know we need each other.

Thank you, dear Lord, for helping me to see myself as others see me, and for the freedom I've gained from that insight.

JoAnn

I AM A MIRACLE

. . . unless this person can experience an entire psychic change, there is very little hope of his recovery.
Dr. William D. Silkworth

Did I need an entire psychic change to get well? Absolutely. In my mind there's no doubt about it. I was one of those hidden housewife drunks known as a closet alcoholic, but I didn't want to look at what I had become. My excuse: I thought I had to drink because I was a nervous wreck and had a number of problems.

Every day I drank from the moment I awoke in the morning until I finally passed out at night. In addition, I took pills - tranquilizers, pain pills, sleeping pills, uppers, downers - anything I could get my hands on.

Since I hid my bottles of vodka under my mattress, I thought no one else knew about my drinking. I lied, wrote bad checks, and stole money from my husband just to keep my supply of booze and pills constant.

The day came when I couldn't go to sleep, or even pass out, no matter how many pills I took or how much booze I drank. Day and night I sat in a chair in my living room and went through a living hell. While I knew I was crazy, I didn't know what to do. If I took more pills or drank any more liquor, I was sure I would die, yet I also knew that I would surely die if I didn't.

After a week of terror the thought occurred to me that maybe I had a drinking problem. In a moment of clarity I could see what I had become and I knew deep down inside that I was, indeed, an alcoholic.

Somehow I staggered to the phone, called the operator and told her that I needed help. Then I sank to the floor and began to cry and plead with God for assistance. Right then and there I turned my life and will over to Him and asked only for His strength and guidance. Instinctively I knew that I could not lick this problem alone and that no human power could relieve my alcoholism.

I was taken to a Recovery House where I was able to get sober and clean. It was there that I was introduced to a program whereby I could learn to live life without alcohol or drugs. It was evident that I had undergone that "psychic change."

For ten years now I have tried to live by God's will for my life instead of my will, and I have been able to live entirely without a drink or a pill. Truly, I am one of those "miracles."

Dear Lord, please help me to always keep my attitude of thankfulness for my personal miracle, the sober life I have been given.

Mary Alice

LIVING WITH
LOSE-LOSE SITUATIONS

To live by the law of Christ and accept him in our hearts is to turn a giant floodlight of hope into our valleys of trouble.
Charles R. Hembree

With an alcoholic, it seems you can never win, but over the years I've discovered that trusting God to lead me provides the strength I need to deal with the lose-lose situations my husband creates.

A prime example is his attitude about my working. When our children were small I stayed home, and my alcoholic husband said that I wasn't contributing enough to the family. I went to work part-time and then he complained that my job and salary were insignificant, and I was neglecting him and the housework. After the children started school I found a full-time job, but he found fault with that too.

On an intellectual level I knew that jealousy and lack of self-worth are often part of an alcoholic's outlook on life. And I knew that my husband's self esteem was so low he saw any change I made as a threat to his world. Unfortunately, recognizing the source of his complaints didn't eliminate my need to deal with them on an emotional level.

I was nervous and unsure about re-entering the working world too, but I also knew I had little choice. My husband's dead end jobs lasted only a few years at a time, until he was fired or he quit, and we needed the stability of a regular income and insurance benefits. Although I was sure that going back to work was the right decision, I still needed reassurance, so I asked the Lord for that as well as for help in making the transition with the least amount of disruption to my family.

My husband ranted and raved, he didn't show up to watch the kids when he knew I had to work late, and he accused me of having affairs with every man in the firm. I cried at first, then tuned him out because I knew his accusations weren't true. And I learned to accept the fact that if he wanted to believe them, he could and would do so regardless of what I said.

Things still aren't easy. I'm often exhausted and I live in fear that my husband will show up at my place of employment and cause embarrassment or put my job in jeopardy. But I have also moved one step closer to separating myself from his problem by putting my own life and the responsibility for our sons first. When my husband is ready to call out for help, I'll be there. In the meantime, my life must go on.

Dearest God, thank you for giving me the inner strength to deal with the lose-lose situations my husband creates.

Jill

A GRATEFUL ALCOHOLIC

It is only when people begin to shake loose from their preconceptions, from the ideas that have dominated them, that we begin to receive a sense of opening, a sense of vision.
Barbara Ward

I couldn't believe what my ears were hearing. There I was at my first AA meeting and some young woman was standing behind the podium, smiling, and telling all of us that she was a grateful alcoholic! Grateful? "You've got to be kidding," I thought, but others obviously understood her feelings for the applause was loud and appreciative for her speech. Well, they could clap if they wanted to, but there wasn't any way I was going to applaud someone who claimed to be grateful that they could no longer drink sanely without making a fool of themselves.

Alcohol had been my only passion in life, and I resented the fact I was forced to give it up. I didn't want to listen to the reasons why these people were grateful, happy and smiling. I didn't want their faith in a higher power. The only thing I wanted was a drink.

But despite my disbelief and anger and that terrible longing for alcohol, I somehow got past those initial months in AA without swallowing that first deadly sip. During that time I attended a lot of meetings and everyone told me to relax, that I'd start to understand things in time. Like so many others before me, I too eventually discovered the truth of our shared experiences.

Alcohol robbed me of my adolescence for I started drinking heavily at 16 and for six long years was drunk almost every day and night. When I sobered up at 22 I was confused and frightened about almost everything. I prayed daily like they told me to, but I had no faith.

Then one day I stopped feeling so scared. While I was driving to the grocery store a wonderful feeling of contentment overwhelmed me. It started from the inside, in my heart, and spread through the rest of my body. The faith that I had lost so many years ago had finally returned and I literally felt it come back. Since that day it has grown steadily and the changes it has brought to my life are immeasurable.

When I was drinking I had no dreams and no hope for the future beyond the next bottle. Now the world has opened up for me and I know I'm a better and stronger person for having gone through this difficult test. Like the young woman who made such an impression on me years ago, I, too, am a grateful alcoholic, and I'm not kidding!

I am grateful for the return of my faith Lord, and ask you to grant me continuing peace and serenity and the wisdom to stay away from alcohol for the rest of my life.

Michelle

IT STARTED WITH PRAYER

If you ask anything in my name, I will do it.
John 14:14 (RSV)

My brother's drinking worries me. I'm afraid he is killing himself with his nightly gin on the rocks. Although he might not start until 9:00 p.m., and although he sips instead of gulping like I always did, Charles continues until he falls asleep, usually after midnight. That's a lot of alcohol, even for a large man.

Daily I pray for his recovery, but I don't even see a hint of concern on his part. When I become discouraged I remember . . . "Margaret," I said to my 12-year-old daughter, "Did you empty this bottle of gin and replace it with water?" "Yes, Mom, I did. I'm afraid you're hurting yourself. I think you're an alcoholic."

We talked about it for a few minutes before I said, more accurately and prophetically than I ever dreamed, "I don't have a problem, but if I did you couldn't do anything about it except to pray."

Actually I was scared too, just not scared enough. Once I attended open AA meetings. For a couple of months I heard men and women share their experiences. While I continued to drink I learned that people play games and realized I had played a few myself. During one period of my life I tried cutting back by using more gin and less water; when that didn't work I reversed the procedure, and when that didn't work I quit trying. And not long after I started, I quit going to AA too.

Two and a half years after that conversation with Margaret I reached my bottom. I was promising myself that I would stop, as I used to, with dinner, but I couldn't. One night at a dinner party everyone but me switched from wine to coffee after the meal, while I kept going to the kitchen and helping myself to the host's liquor. Embarrassed and full of fear, a couple of weeks later, for the first time ever, I asked my prayer group to pray for me. Shame filled me. Helplessness overwhelmed me. Still, I didn't know if I really wanted to quit.

"The prayers won't work," I said. But they did. In the following days I was sustained by a new peace and by what I'd learned in AA eight years earlier, to focus on one day at a time and to tell God thank you each night for sobriety.

Later I learned my friends had been concerned about my drinking and praying for me for many months before I had asked for help, so perhaps my brother's recovery has already begun because of my prayers for him.

Help me, Lord, to trust and be patient as others were when they prayed for me.

Patricia

IT CAN'T BE FIXED

In one brief love-kissed moment, you did keep your God appointed destiny to rise in mortal flesh.
Connie Huggins

> Like a child who brings her broken toy with
>   tears for Dad to mend,
> I held my broken child, now dead, and stared
>   at my best friend.
> "It can't be fixed," I heard him say, "now turn
>   and walk away."
> I screamed and wept to no avail. That day was
>   Judgment Day.

We'd been fighting since noon - my husband, the alcoholic and me, the enabler. More than sorrow, there was anger and hate and disappointment directed toward this man who'd been sober for three months until yesterday.

Yesterday, we drove the icy roads to see relatives and I knew he would drink. He always drank heavily with his brother and I went along "to help; to keep him under control; to be his savior."

Coming home through the pass he lost control of the car and we hit the mountain wall with such force that our two-and-a-half month old baby was crushed against the front windshield. Our tiny son was dead before he'd had a chance to throw a ball or run a race, to develop his personality and skills, or make his mark in the world.

Or did he?

Without his brief journey through our lives, would we now be so aware of our weaknesses and helplessness?

If his weeping had not echoed in the night, would my tears ever have fallen on light?

If the warmth of his little body had never been nestled close to my breast, would I sense his hand in mine leading me through forgiveness to hope?

He paid the price for sobriety and healing for my husband and me and our desire is to honor the gift and the Giver.

That tiny babe finished his race - so soon a winner. May he wait for us in peace as our race now begins.

Please hold my other hand, Dear God, I can't do this alone.

Lisa

A POSITIVE VIEW OF SUFFERING

Those who are fully alive are also usually those who have been deeply wounded, and the God who came to us in Jesus of Nazareth was fully alive, with an awareness and a joy and a perceptiveness most of us can only wonder at. Along with the joy was a willingness to assume all of our human sufferings, which should make us look differently at our own pain.

Madeline L'Engle

It was hard to tell her about myself because my drinking has always been such a closely guarded secret. Now, if I wanted to help this girl, I knew I must tell her my story. Uneasily I perched on the side of her bed, breathed deeply, and took the plunge.

"I had my first drink when I was 17," I began, and felt my stomach tighten. "Alcohol relaxed me and I began to rely on it more and more." My hands were getting cold. By the time I got to the part where I, too, had been hospitalized for alcoholism, I was tense all over. After years of shame-induced secrecy, here I was, forcing myself to tell everything to this young stranger.

Her dark shadowed eyes seemed too big for such a small face. She stared up at me. "You look so good," she whispered wistfully. "You made it, didn't you? Do you really think I can make it too?"

"Yes, with God's help," I affirmed - and suddenly I felt overwhelmed by the miracle of my own recovery. Self-concern disappeared. Gratitude took its place. I reached for her hand and added, "With God's help, and the help of your many new friends, you will make it too."

Secrets? Never again. For on that day I learned that suffering is my greatest asset. It enables me to see into the hearts of hurting human beings, feel their pain, and walk beside them until, together, we stand in the bright light of a new and wonderful sobriety.

Thank you, Lord, for using me to help others and for being there to help us all.

Doris

FAITH DIDN'T MAKE MY LIFE EASIER

Believers have as many difficulties as sceptics. In fact they often find a failure harder to bear.

Dr. Paul Tournier

My wife Susan was a very talented and successful woman, but she didn't believe in herself, and my efforts to convince her of her self worth failed.

It was a second marriage for both of us. She successfully hid her alcoholism from me during the months we were dating. Sometimes when we went to a nice restaurant she'd have a drink before dinner or a glass of wine with her meal, but never more than one. It was only after we became husband and wife that I found out how much alcohol she was actually consuming.

Despite her penchant for the bottle, we were very happy the first few months of our life together. The honeymoon phase ended when we disagreed over her teen-aged daughter's behavior. I could not believe that she would allow a 16-year-old girl to be out drinking 3.2 beer with her friends until 3:00 a.m., and she couldn't understand why I saw anything wrong with what the girl was doing.

When her daughter's behavior drove a wedge of friction between us that threatened our marriage, my wife agreed to go with me for counselling. I thought if Susan would quit drinking herself, she'd be able to think rationally, and would see what a terrible example she was setting for her child. Unfortunately, it didn't work that way.

From the beginning, our pastor made it clear to me that there was absolutely nothing I could do to make Susan stop drinking. She would have to do that herself. On one level of consciousness I heard what he was saying and realized he had had enough experience working with alcoholics to know what he was talking about. But on another level I still thought there must be something I could do to help.

Like most men my age I had been raised to believe that it was my responsibility to take care of my wife and protect her from all harm. Because I felt that included protecting her from herself, I had a terrible time accepting my pastor's comments on a gut level. Part of me just refused to believe I couldn't provide the help she needed, so I kept on frantically praying for assistance.

When Susan's drinking progressed to the point that she began having blackouts while driving, she confided in her supervisor who immediately came to me with that information. I interpreted my wife's confession as a plea for help and thought an intervention at this point might be an answer to my prayers. It seemed to me that if we got together a group of friends and relatives who loved her, and all confronted her about her drinking at once, saying that we would do what we could to help her stop, that it might make a difference.

Well it did make a difference, but not the way I had hoped. Instead of the beginning of a cure, it turned out to be the beginning of the end for us as a couple, and ultimately we divorced despite the fact I still loved her.

A couple years later Susan and I tried to start over again. Her daughter had married and moved away and I naively thought maybe that was the incentive my ex-wife needed to change. But I quickly discovered it hadn't made any difference. She was still consuming an enormous volume of alcohol every night after she came home from work.

And so we said good-by again, but that time it was final.

Talking through my experiences for this meditation was very tough for me because it dredged up old memories that are easier to live with when I try to forget them. I still struggle with the fact that I couldn't help my wife and that my prayers for Susan weren't answered. But I've also learned a lot about alcoholism and about myself in the years since our marriage disintegrated.

When I first discovered my wife was an alcoholic, I thought my faith would provide quick solutions to her drinking problem. When that didn't happen I felt like a failure as it seemed to me that she would surely have been healed if I had just prayed harder, or more, or differently. While I now doubt that changing the intensity or frequency of my prayers would have radically altered what happened, I suspect that changing the nature of them might at least have changed me and my responses.

When I am tempted to blame myself, God, help me to realize that your ways are not our ways and that what feels like failure here may not be so at all.

William

LIVING WITH ANGER;
TAMING MY RAGE

Be angry but do not sin; do not let the sun go down on your anger.
Ephesians 4:26 (RSV)

Living with an alcoholic produced a great deal of anger in me until I discovered he wasn't the loser in that exchange; I was.

I used to lay in bed at night doing a slow burn as I mentally reviewed the events of the day. When it comes right down to it, there were many things I had a right to be angry about. Intellectually I know that anger in itself isn't wrong. But the problems came, not from the anger, but from what I did with it.

When left to fester, my anger was a very destructive emotion. Not only did it cause me to do and say things I often regretted later, it turned me into a hostile person.

Perhaps it would have been different if my anger had just been focused on my alcoholic spouse, but it wasn't. It spilled over into all my other relationships as well. Far too often I lashed out at my child or snapped at co-workers and friends for no apparent reason.

I told myself I had to live life one day at a time and yet, I insisted on carrying my anger around for days or weeks on end. No matter how justified my anger was, I found I had to get rid of it each night or I woke up even more hostile the next morning.

So now instead of lying in bed at night fuming, I've learned to pour my heart out to God and tell Him all about my day, including what made me angry and why. Releasing my anger to God and leaving my frustrations with Him helps me to resolve my emotional turmoil. I go to sleep in peace, knowing that when I awake I'll be able to start my day off on the right foot, free from the hostilities of the day before.

I don't have to let my anger warp my feelings for my husband or my relationships with others. But most important, I don't have to let it ruin me.

Thank you, Lord, for absorbing the anger I've shared with you and for helping me to live successfully a day at a time.

Melanie

I'M TURNING OUT O.K.

A lot of us . . . have had unhappy or strange childhoods, but this need not be lethally crippling.
                    Madeleine L'Engle

I'll never forget the times my father threw me out of his house. And though that was bad enough, it hurt even more to realize that he didn't see my tears. Nor did he realize the humiliation I suffered when I begged him to let me stay because I had nowhere else to go.

Even now he's not aware of how his drinking has affected me and my ability to relate to others. Nor does he know of the agony I've dumped on the laps of numerous counselors.

But I've lived through it all and I'm turning out okay. My life has been altered by the way he has treated me, but it hasn't been destroyed. Though my childhood was rough and I often dreamed of escaping it, I've learned I can leave it behind.

From the depths of the deprivation I faced in those growing up years, God made something beautiful. So little can mean so much to one who has had nothing. I am thankful for the perspectives He has given me. Although many people don't know how fortunate they are, I do, for He taught me to see the value of everyday kindnesses.

When someone holds my hand, tears of happiness fill my eyes. That person is filling a need of mine that wasn't touched in my younger years.

When a friend listens to what I have to say and then tells me he's proud of me or impressed by my accomplishments, my heart sings. Feeling appreciated is sheer bliss for me.

And when I hold my own small son in my arms and tell him that I love him (something I never heard as a child), my life fills up with joy. I have a reason for being. I am needed, I am loved, and I am okay despite the fact I had an alcoholic father.

Thank you, Father, for helping me to overcome my past.
                    Pamela

GIVING UP THE JUDGE'S GAVEL

A man's judgment of another depends more on the one judging and on his passions than on the one being judged and his conduct.
Dr. Paul Tournier

Though I never pictured myself sitting on the bench and declaring my fellow man guilty with a rap of my gavel, I spent a good many years of my life portraying that role. How many times when I was drinking, did I judge my activities, my companions, and the place where I was to be evil? How long I spent in judgment of people, places and things, and all to no avail.

It has taken many years of sobriety in the program of Alcoholics Anonymous for me to begin to see that God is not limited to my finite concepts. My judgments of my fellow humans, of my circumstances, of my location, make no difference whatsoever in the larger scheme of things. My judgments only have the power to upset me.

I was at an A.A. meeting, when a fellow I had never seen before was called on to speak. The subject was tolerance. He spoke for a few moments, generally telling a part of his story. As he spoke, I judged him. I was checking out his manner of speech, his clothing, and his background - judging them against my own concept of what I knew to be o.k. As his story went on, I had all but dismissed him from consideration when he got to the point.

Like a rocket, his words screamed by my ears: "I found that in spite of my judgments, God loved me. He loved me when I was drunk. He loves me in my sobriety. And he will love me in spite of what I do with the rest of my life. Working to spread the message of A.A., which is the message of God in a non-judgmental way, is my way of showing my love of God."

All of a sudden, I was able to see my life clearly. I felt a warmth spreading inside of me and experienced a certainty that I had never felt before. My fears left me and I felt complete. There was no longer any need to run from my past, be ashamed of the places I had frequented, or judgmental of my companions of yesterday or today.

It was clear that God loved me despite everything I had ever been and everything that I had ever done and there was nothing I could ever do to change that fact. And when I finally accepted that fact in my heart, and in my brains, and in my gut, I was able to put away my judge's gavel and get on with my life.

God, help me to know today and tomorrow and every day, that nothing needs my judgment to exist.

Ed

THE GLASS CRUTCH

Alcoholism does not come in bottles. It comes in people.
Ann Landers

There are those who believe that alcoholics are made, not born. Then there are others, like myself, who believe that our inherited nervous, mental and emotional make-up have much to do with addiction.

When I was only a few months old, my young mother killed herself during a postpartum depression by leaping down a country well. My father, a frail, high-strung man, died of pneumonia at the age of 30. Because of that history, I have always believed that the seeds of alcoholism were with me from the very beginning.

In his book, MAN AGAINST HIMSELF, Dr. Karl Menninger states that alcoholism is not a disease, but a flight from a disease. All alcoholics are fleeing from something, if only from responsibility or boredom. I was fleeing from things I couldn't identify, shadows and apprehensions that made me miserably uncomfortable in a world full of people who appeared to be perfectly at ease.

Then I discovered alcohol, the magic fix. It calmed my nerves, quieted my fears, and allowed me to move comfortably in the real world - for awhile.

But in time the magic fix became even more frightening than the mysterious shadows and fears, and the day finally came when I was forced to give up booze and its terrible consequences.

God and I were not well acquainted, but I had heard of Him. I wasn't an agnostic or an atheist, but neither was I a practicing believer. Not knowing where else to turn for help, I began to pray, and in a most miraculous way God worked through sober alcoholics, who led me to Alcoholics Anonymous.

Today I can face life without the glass crutch. Oh, there are still times, under certain circumstances, when I am extremely ill at ease. But now, if I feel too uncomfortable, I just go home. There are simpler ways of fighting shadows than drinking myself into insensibility.

Though the experts recognize alcoholism when they see it, they still don't agree on what causes it. But does it really matter? Our bodies and minds are unique. We must all work with what God has given us, and if we ask Him, He will show us the way.

Thank you, God, for enabling me to throw away the glass crutch.

Nancy

GOODBY, WONDER WOMAN

An important part of our recovery is finding out who we really are - not who we have been told we should be, not who we think we should be.
Anne Wilson Schaef

To the outside world, I looked like a "wonder woman" - an intelligent, attractive female with a family and a career. Unfortunately, the inside didn't match the outside.

Perhaps I was afraid of authority figures and angry people because I was raised in an alcoholic home and married to a recovering alcoholic. On occasion I accepted abuse and minimized it by saying, "It wasn't that bad. If I try harder, next time he won't get mad." Despite my rationalizing, I often felt trapped and unable to assert myself appropriately, just like the kid years ago who faced an irrational parent.

Frequently I didn't take reasonable care of myself, for everybody else's needs were more important than my own. Mistakenly, I felt responsible for other people's feelings and attitudes and, of course, if I didn't keep the other person happy, I was sure it was all my fault.

How did I get out of that rut and turn myself around? What convinced me that being wonder woman wouldn't solve all my problems?

My one word answer would have to be "prayer." In my pain, I begged God to help me and He sent a loved one who realized I needed to see myself differently. I thought I had hidden everything behind the facade I presented, but my sister saw beneath my disguise a hurting woman who desperately needed help despite my academic awards and superior evaluations. She took me to AlAnon and there I learned to "adopt" that confused child inside me and nurture her.

Going to those meetings also gave me the courage to go to Family Court, and that was a major victory for me, for being a victim today is a choice, not a necessity. As suggested, my children have attended an educational series on alcoholism, and we are all in family therapy. Hopefully, my children won't become "victims of victims."

Thanks to the help I received there, I hung up my "professional rescuer" badge and today I can take care of others without neglecting myself or enabling others to be irresponsible. Our family recovery from alcoholism and co-dependency has been painstakingly slow with many setbacks like depression and unemployment, but God has given our family the tools of AA, Al-Anon and therapy, and He is helping us build anew.

Thank you, Father, for enabling me to recognize and tend to my own needs, and for the freedom and direction that has given me.

Suzanne

FORGIVENESS CAN TAKE A LIFETIME

To err is human, to forgive divine.
Alexander Pope

My father started drinking after he became addicted to pain medication with a high alcohol content. He might have been another Billy Graham if it hadn't been for his accident. Dad was a minister with a gift for words that landed him a tall steeple pastorate at a very young age. At a time when most men are just beginning their climb to success, he reached the pinnacle of his, but he fell from that mountain top as quickly as he climbed it and through no fault of his own.

An accident left him in such severe pain that he couldn't function without continual medication. While that dosage might not have bothered someone with a different physiological makeup, in no time at all dad became an addict; then he turned to liquor and became an alcoholic. Shortly thereafter he was forced to resign his pastorate because of "ill health." That feeble explanation avoided embarrassment for the church and public disgrace for my father, but it was just a band-aid solution for our family because it temporarily kept us together.

After a period of treatment and rest, Dad convinced us that he had his alcoholism under control and accepted the call of a church in another city. My mother, brother and I looked forward with some reservation to this new beginning. For a short while everything went well; my father seemed to be his old self again and there was no evidence he was drinking. But within a year we all realized that he was imbibing secretly and slipping back into his old ways.

His drinking ceased to be a family secret when several newspaper articles made his drinking problem a public fact. His final humiliation and disgrace came on a Sunday evening when he tried to lead a service while he was drunk.

I felt betrayed and left the church in a pain-filled rage because I wanted no more of him in my life. For that outrageous performance he was tried in the courts of his denomination for conduct unbecoming a pastor, stripped of his credentials, and forced to leave the ministry.

During the next fifteen years I had very little contact with my father. He wrote to me but I didn't reply. When I learned that he had found sobriety through Alcoholics Anonymous and had been reinstated into the ministry, I was skeptical because I still expected to hear that his "magic bubble" had burst.

My father died in 1956 of a massive heart seizure. Even as I attended his funeral with his second wife, I wondered how sincere and complete his rehabilitation had been. Although I knew it hurt my father deeply, I had never been able to completely forgive him.

Twenty years later, after I retired, my wife and I visited my stepmother. I had not seen her since my father's funeral. She asked me then if I wanted some of Dad's photographs, letters and other memorabilia. Among these was a tape of a speech my father made at the closing session of the Regional Conference of Alcoholics Anonymous in New Orleans in 1952.

When I played that tape, the effect it had on me was overwhelming. Here for the first time, I heard my father telling the story of his life as a minister, as an alcoholic sunk to the gutters, and of his come-back through A.A. He told everything; there were no secrets he didn't share. His speech was tragic, funny, incredulous and sublime. It was as though he was telling me what I had refused to hear or believe for so long.

Great floods of tears and emotions swept over me. Slowly I came to realize the great influence for good that my father had become in his reinstated ministry and with other alcoholics in A.A. In time I came to terms with this great tragedy in my life. And finally I forgave my father and, in turn, received God's forgiveness for my stubborn refusal to believe that He could make a new person out of an alcoholic.

And, at last I am at peace with my father.

Thank you, Lord, for spinning me around to face the great truth that You can do wondrous things and grant peace that passes all understanding.

Willard

Please send me the following books:

_____ copies of **MEDITATIONS FOR
BEREAVED PARENTS**   @ $6.95 each = $ _____

_____ copies of **MEDITATIONS FOR THE
WIDOWED**   @ $6.95 each = $ _____

_____ copies of **MEDITATIONS FOR THE
DIVORCED**   @ $6.95 each = $ _____

_____ copies of **MEDITATIONS FOR THE
TERMINALLY ILL AND THEIR
FAMILIES**   @ $6.95 each = $ _____

_____ copies of **MEDITATIONS FOR
ALCOHOLICS AND THEIR
FAMILIES**   @ $6.95 each = $ _____

                        SUBTOTAL $ _____

For orders of 10 or more books, subtract 10%. $ _____

Add $1.50 shipping costs for the first book and
.25 cents for each additional book to the same address. $ _____

Add $1.50 for each additional shipping address. $ _____
                (Gilgal will include a gift card in
                each shipment to a separate address.)
                        TOTAL DUE $ _____
        Call (503) 593-8418 to place VISA or MasterCard orders.
Ship to: Name _____

          Address _____

          City/State/Zip_____

Gift Address

Ship to: Name _____

          Address _____

          City/State/Zip_____

          Name of sender for gift card _____

Mail order form to: Gilgal Publications
                      P.O. Box 3399
                      Sunriver, OR 97707 USA